Ethereal

The Art of Christopher Micheal Creath

Attempting to Understand Paradise

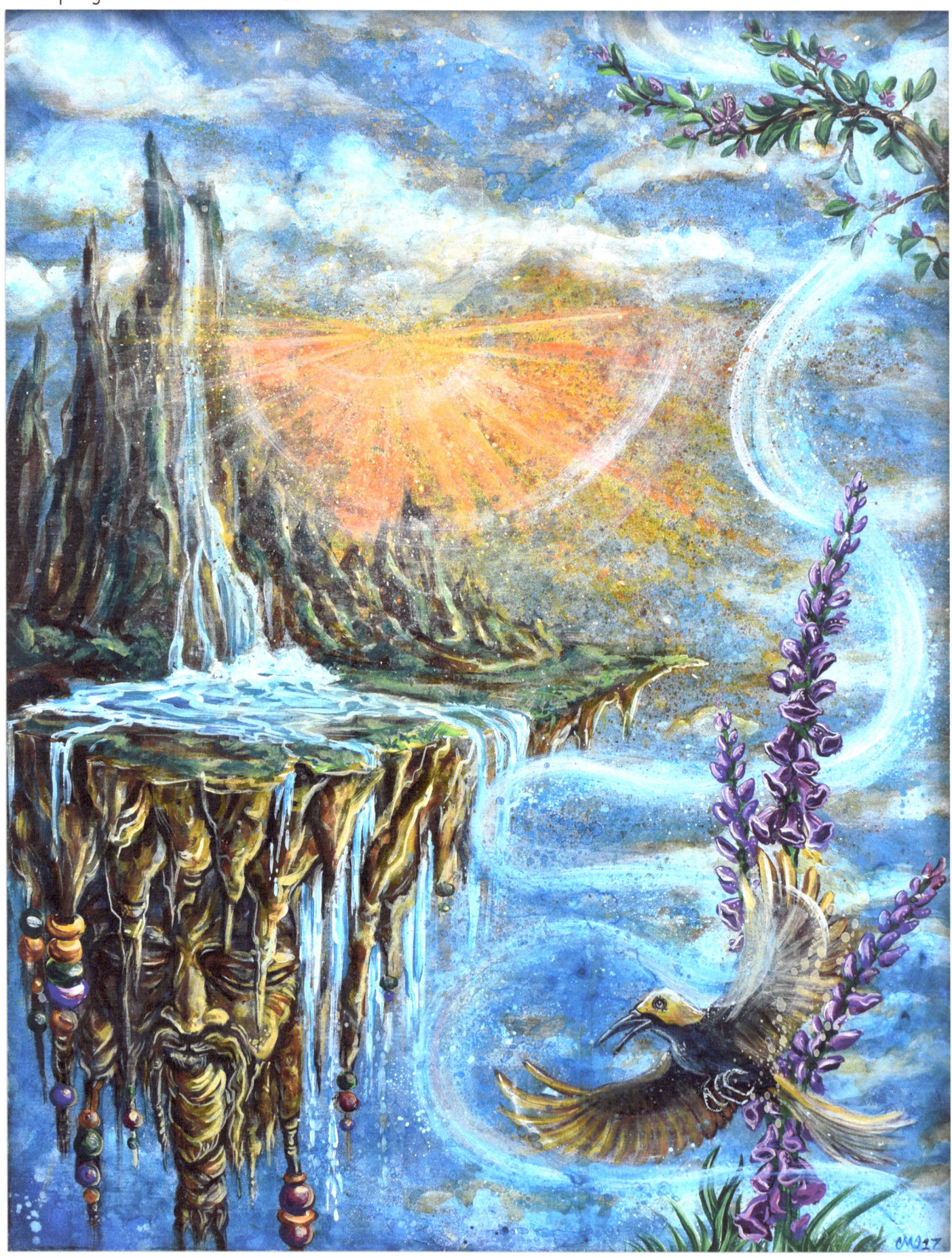

Meditating on what makes the good things good, and whether these things are even meant to be understood.
Acrylic and spraypaint on wood 16"x20"

Cultivating Community

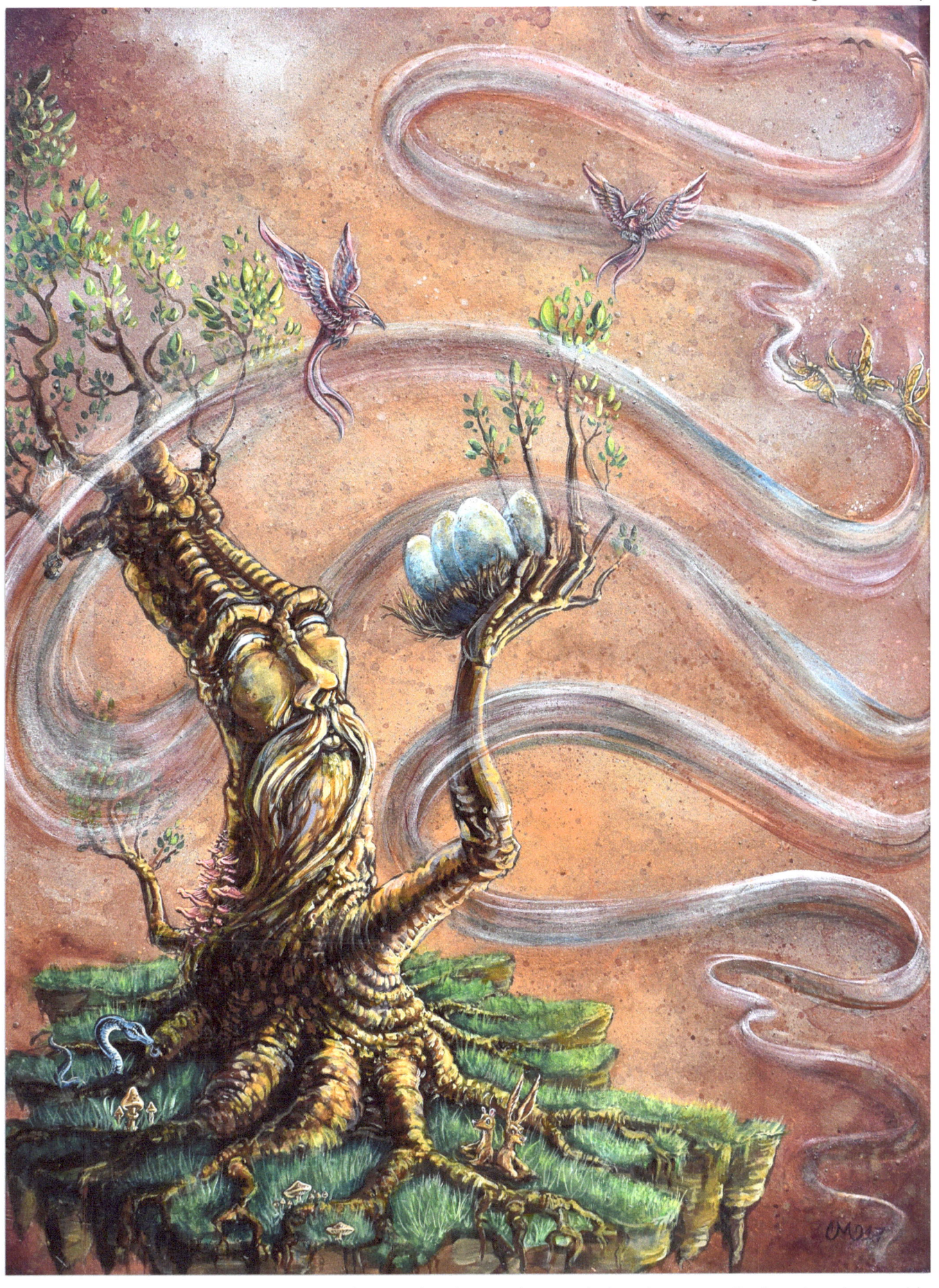

Creating a community where multitudes can thrive. Including those typically thought to be at odds.
Acrylic and spraypaint on wood 18"x24"

Empath

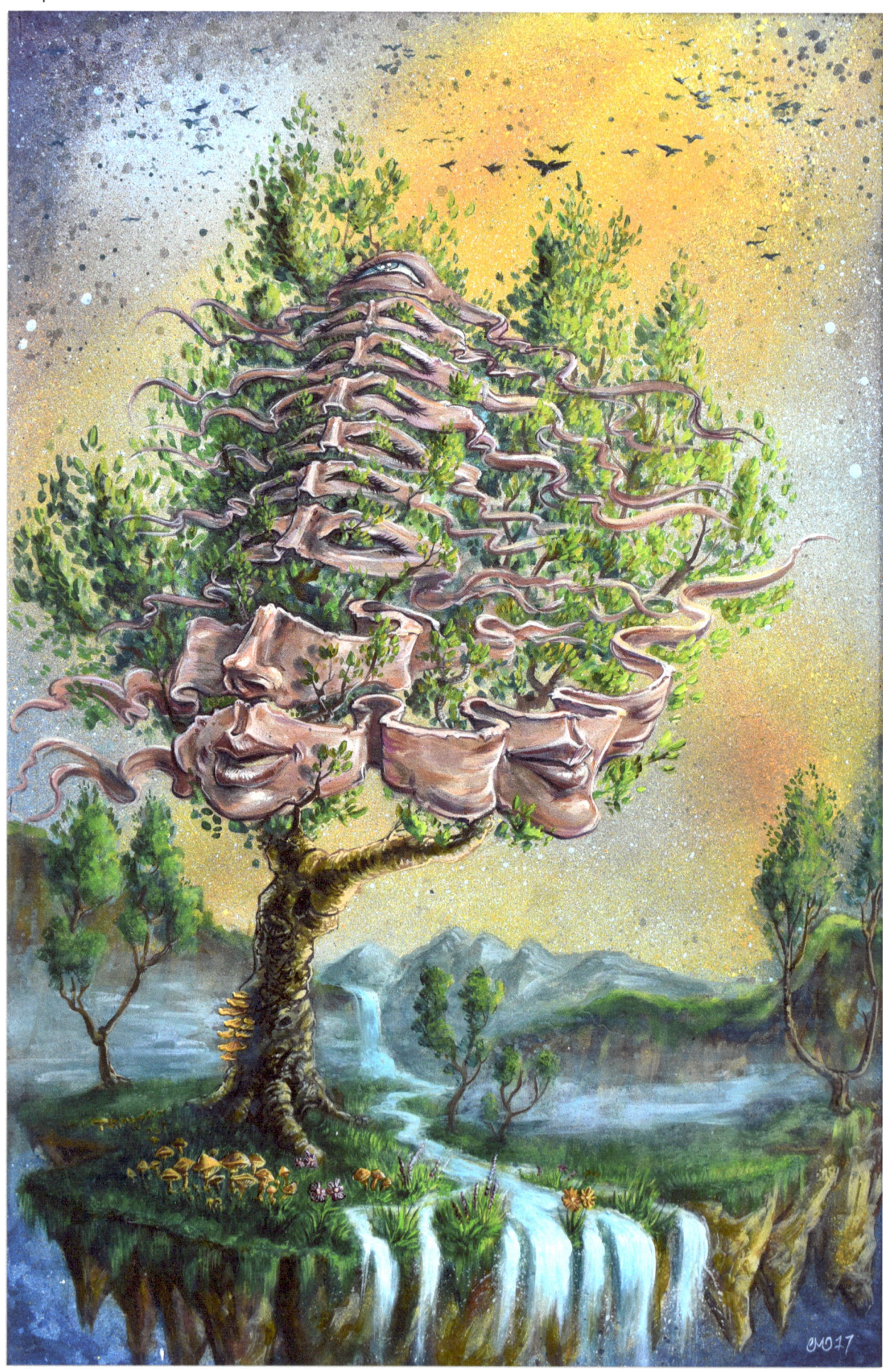

Finding the connection with nature and our environment that allows for a expanded perspective.
Acrylic on wood 16"x24"

Cultivating The Light Inside

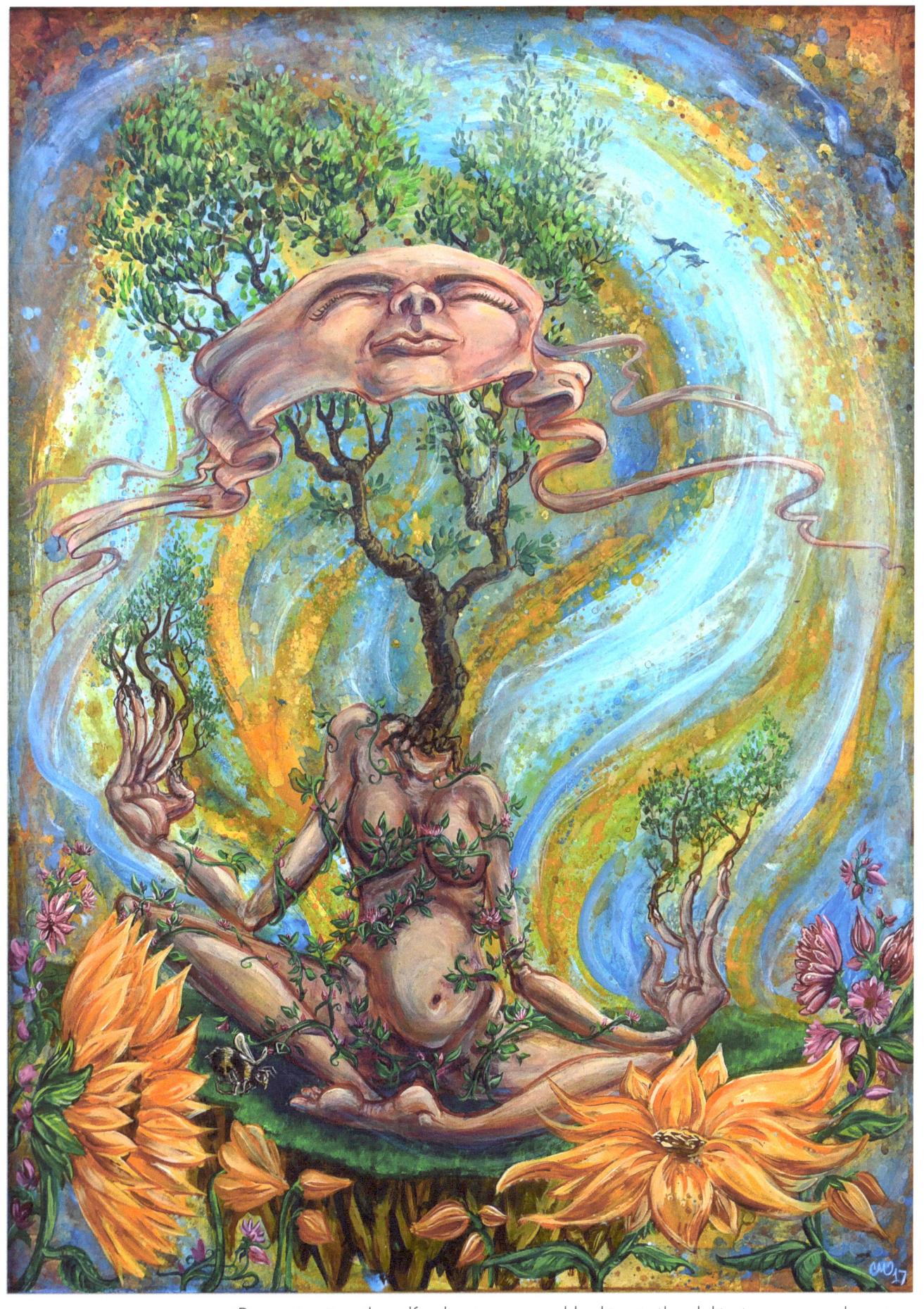

Deconstructing the self, releasing ego and basking in the ability to grow our happiness.
18"x 24" Acrylic on wood

Sea Change

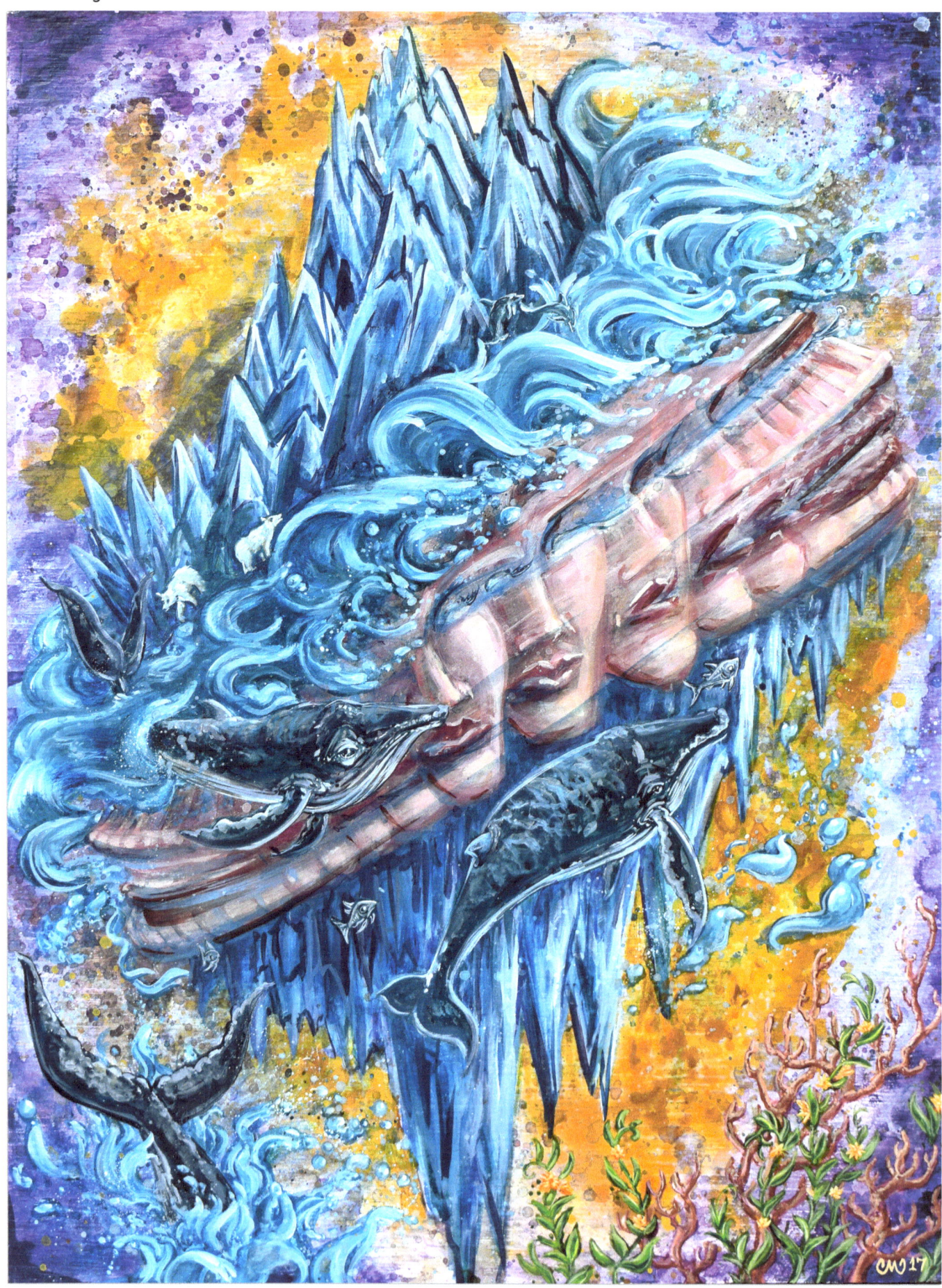

The ever changing tide.
Acrylic on wood 16"x20"

Retaining Wonder

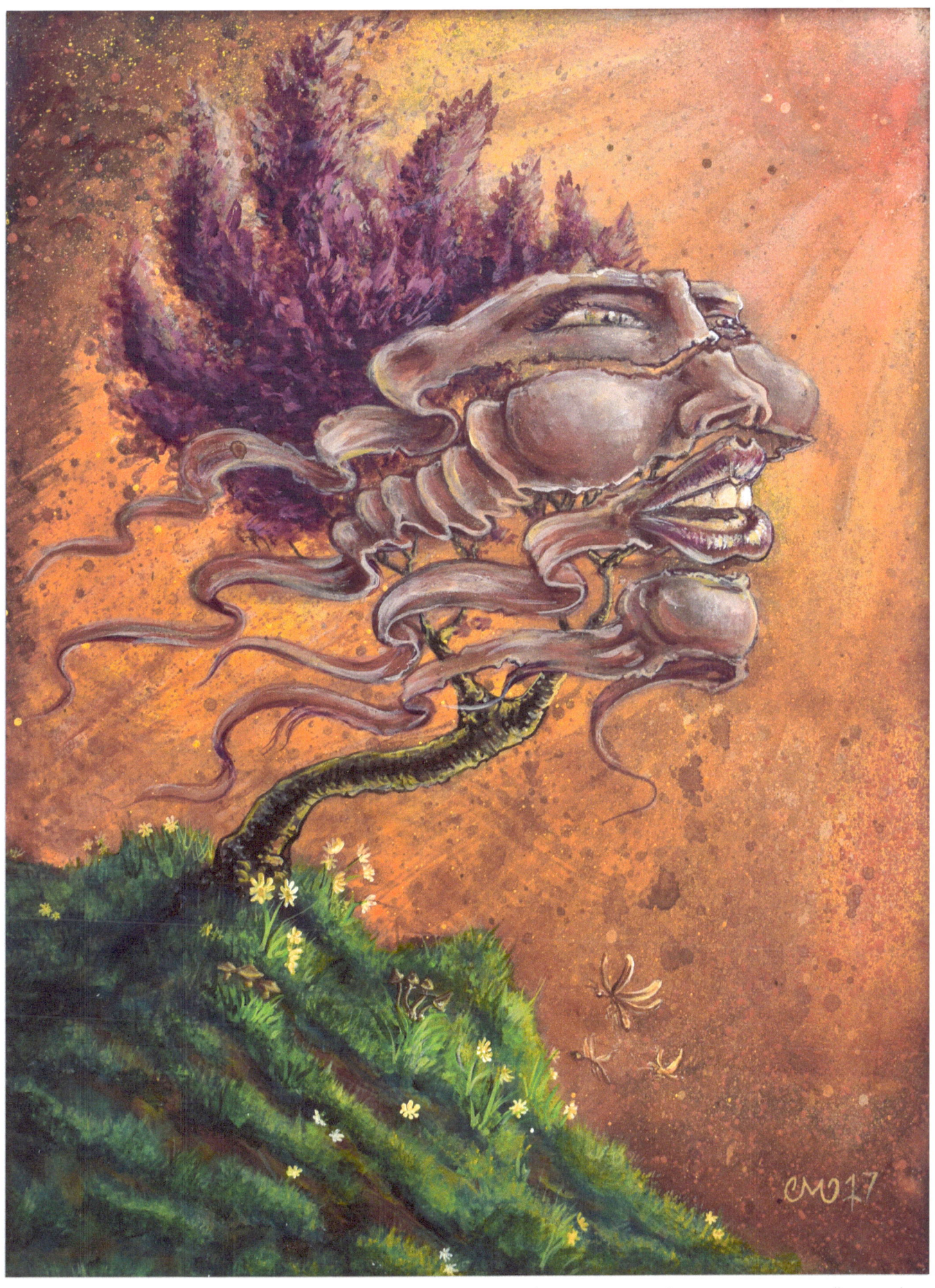

Wonder, so easily lost to time and experience. Magical, awe inspiring phenomenon remain all around us.
Acrylic and spray paint 9"x12"

Illuminated Insight

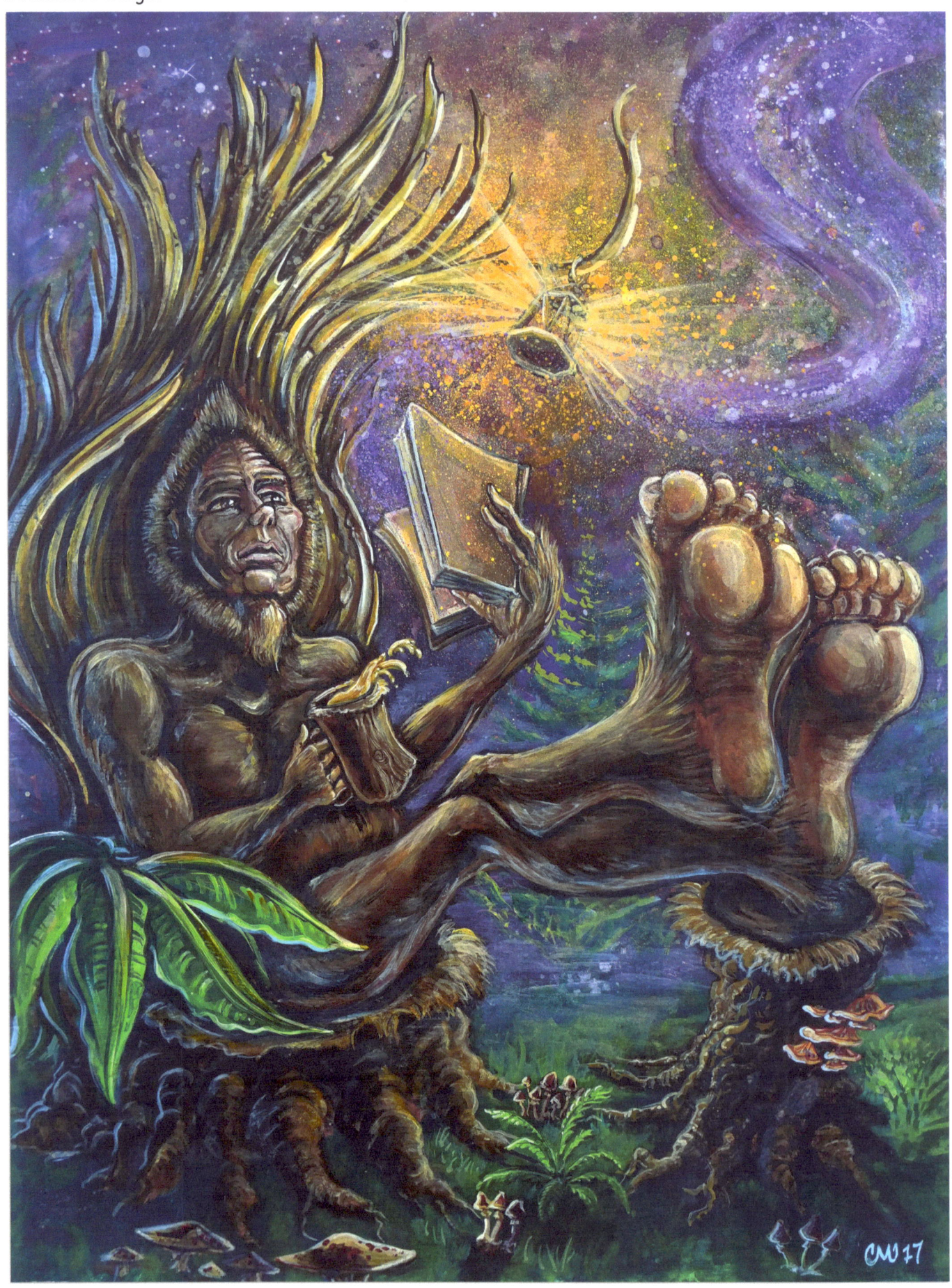

A sophisticated beast on a quest for knowledge.
Acrylic on wood 18"x24"

What She Awakens

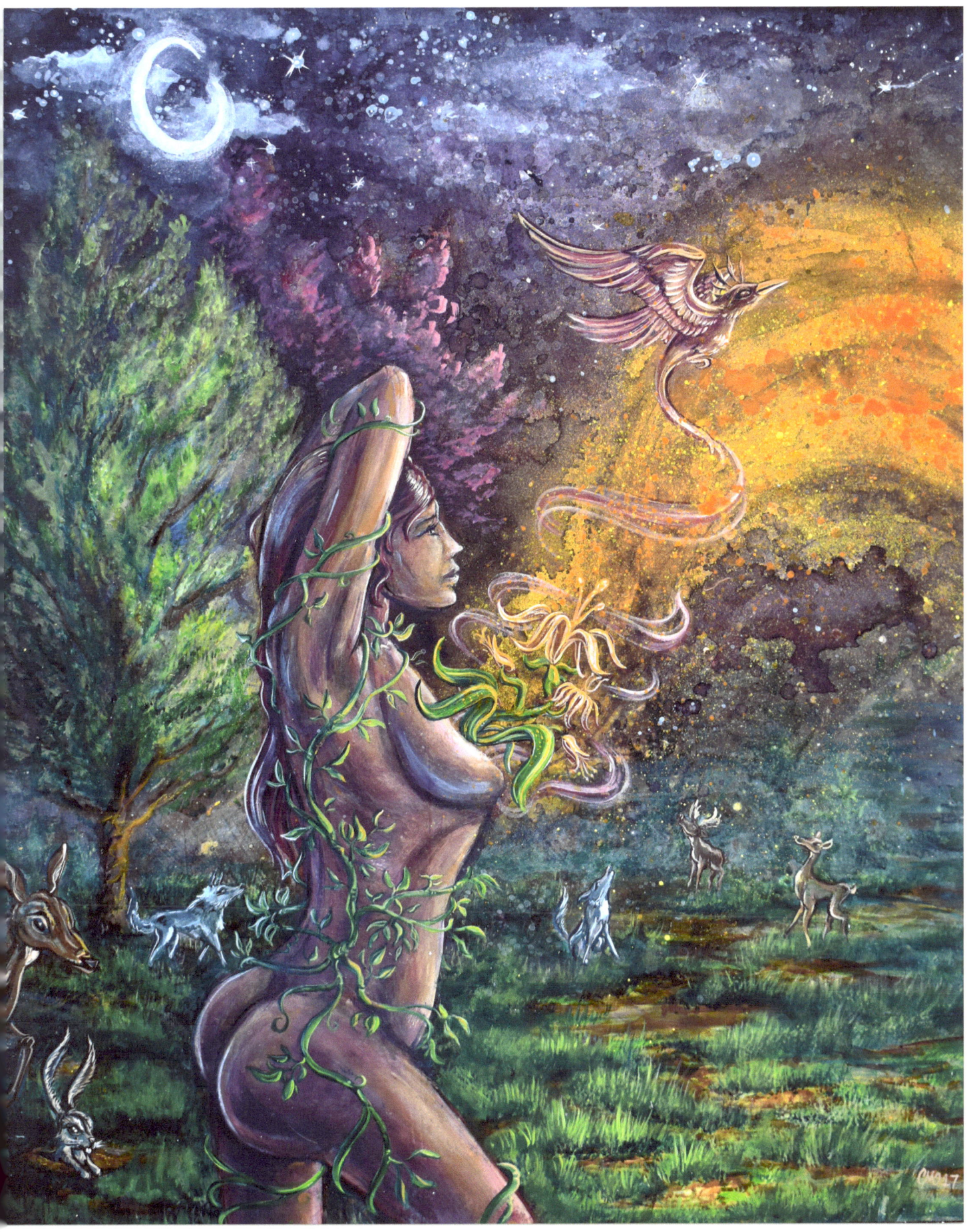

All the good she awakens in me. Thank you special lady.
Acrylic and spray paint on wood 16"x20"

Quantum Superposition

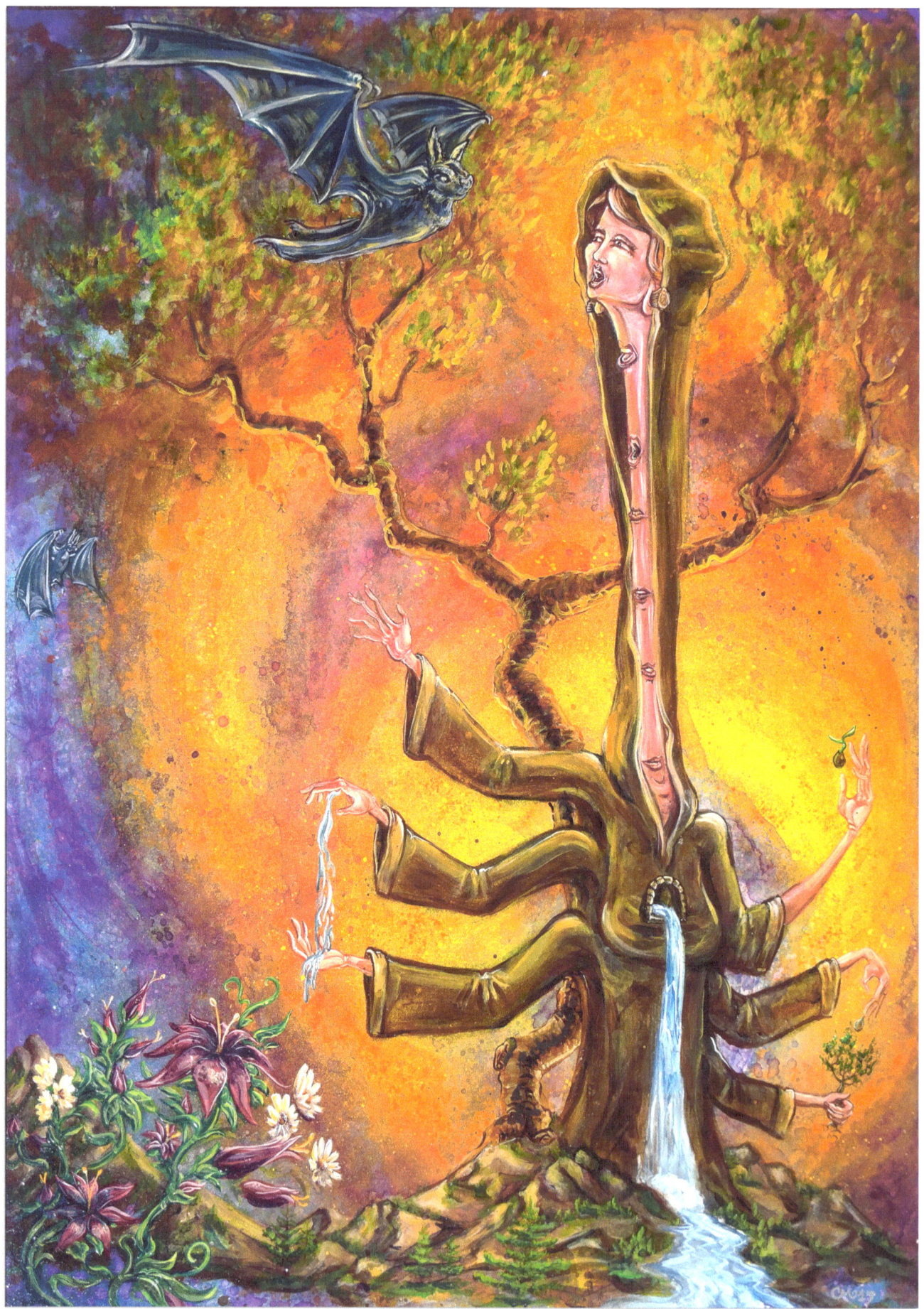

Existing in multiple states simultaneously. Aspiring, giving, and receiving. Nurturing, sowing and harvesting.
Acrylic and spray paint on wood 16"x24"

Tuning Out The Trivial

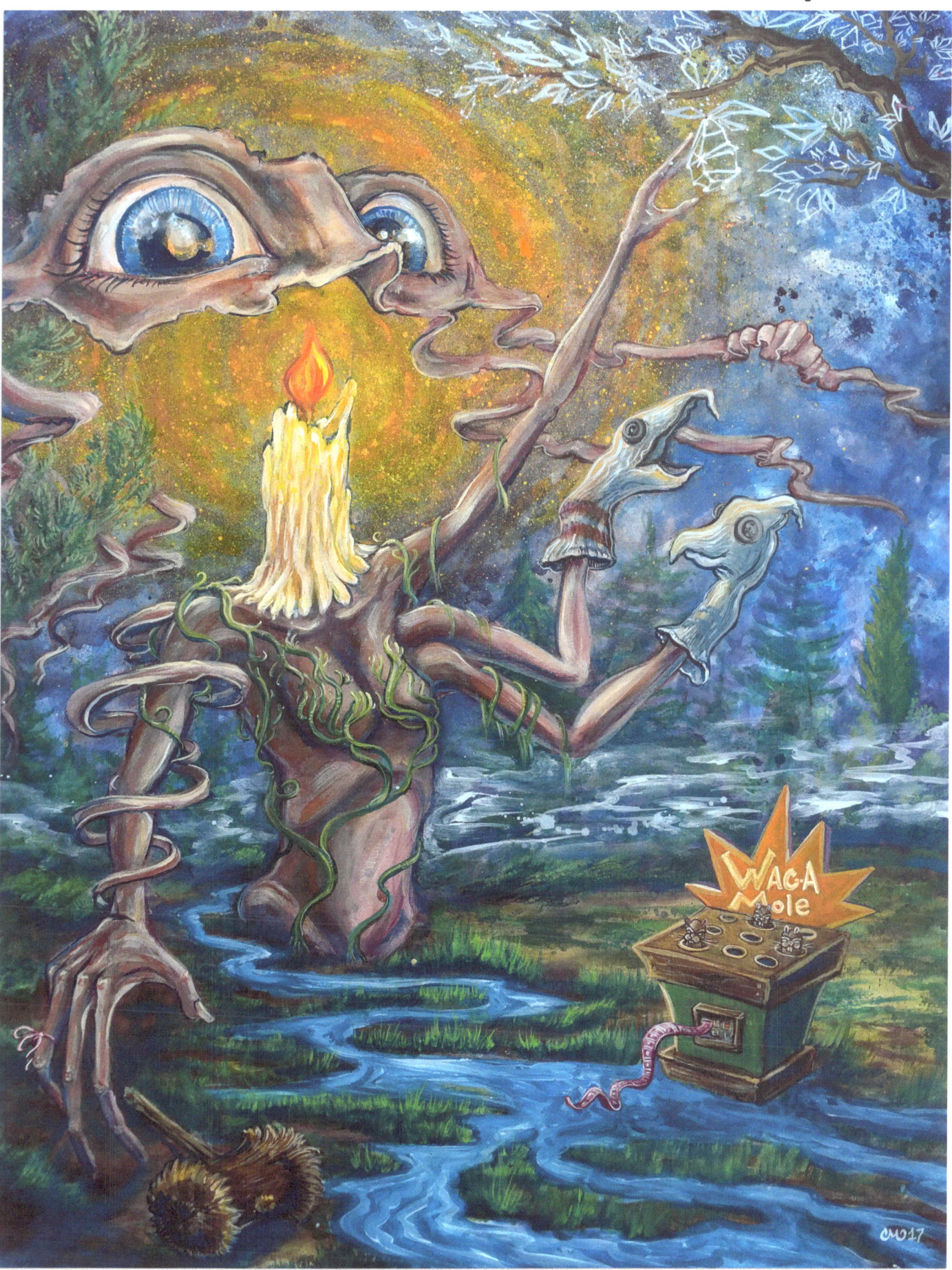

The candle, her motivation, she reaches for an ethereal fruit, her, aspirations. The puppets, everyday drama not positivley adding to her life. The existential Wac-A-Mole, once this problem is handled everything will be perfect from now on... Oh wait there's more!

Acrylic on wood 18"x24"

Tell me a Story

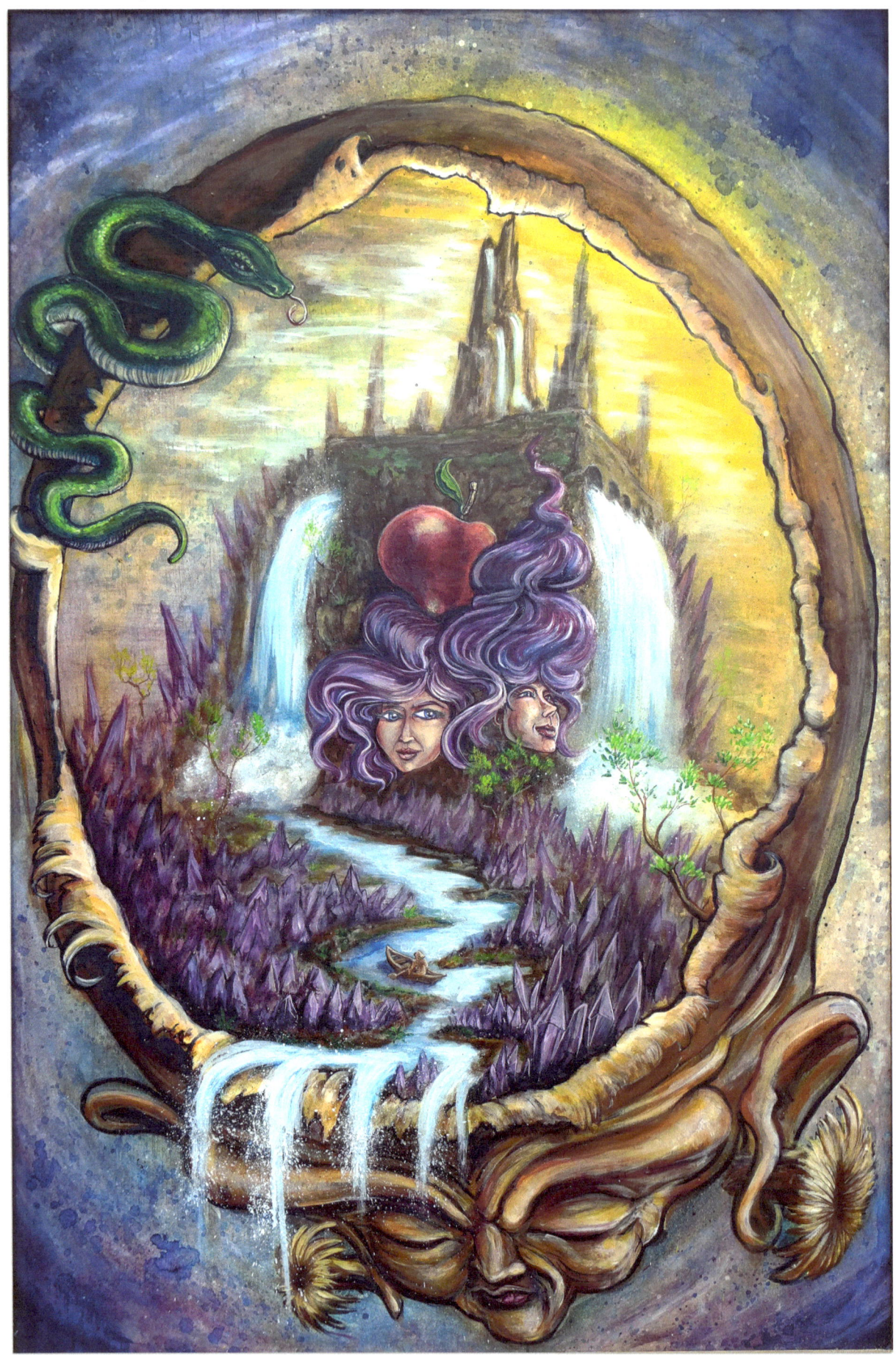

Setting off on an expedition in search of unseen rewards. How do you see the story?
Acrylic on wood 24"x36"

Fly, Love, Read

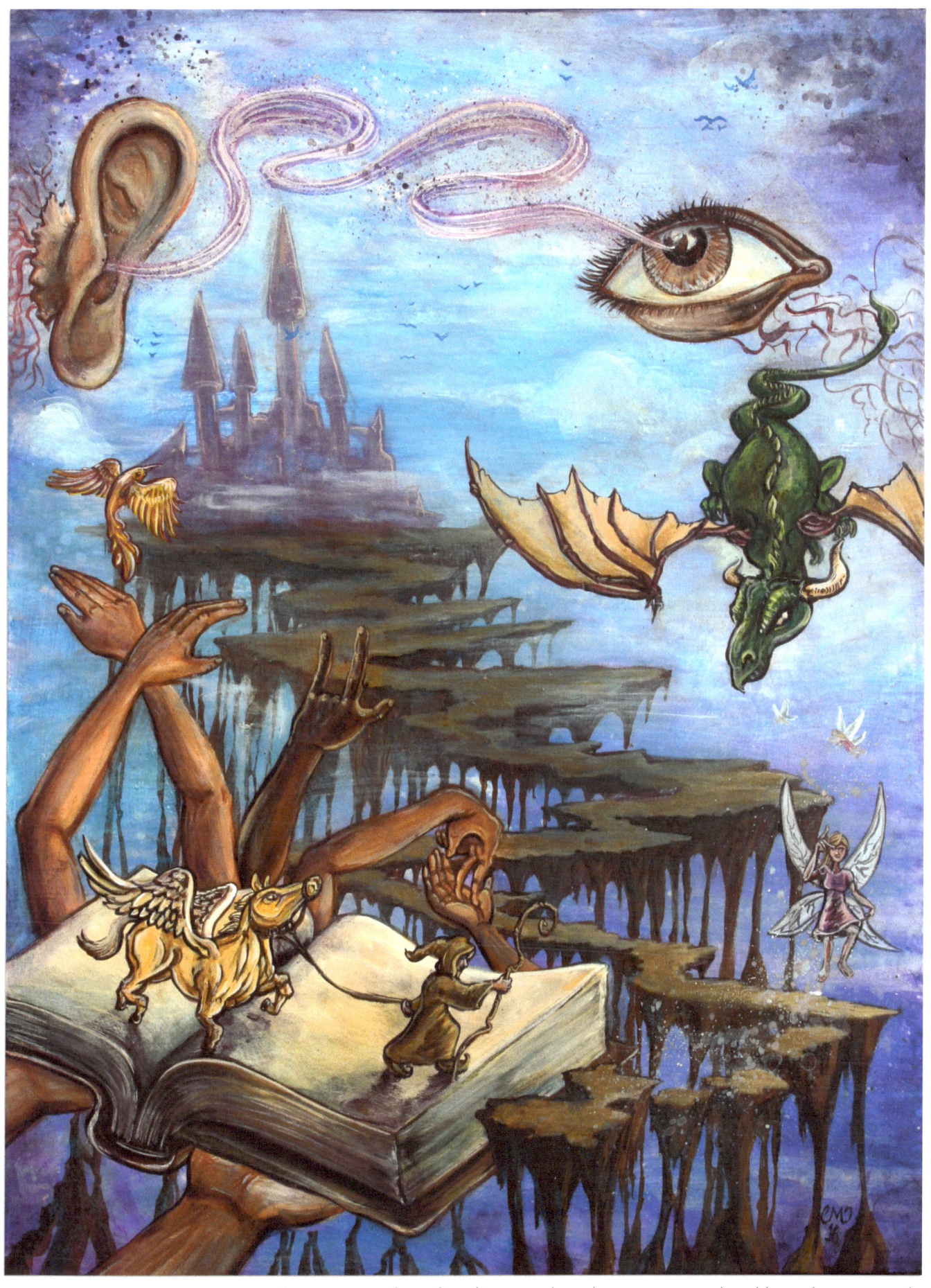

A commission for a friend's niece, she is hearing impaired and loves fantasy novels.
Acrylic on wood 16"x20"

Waves of Creation

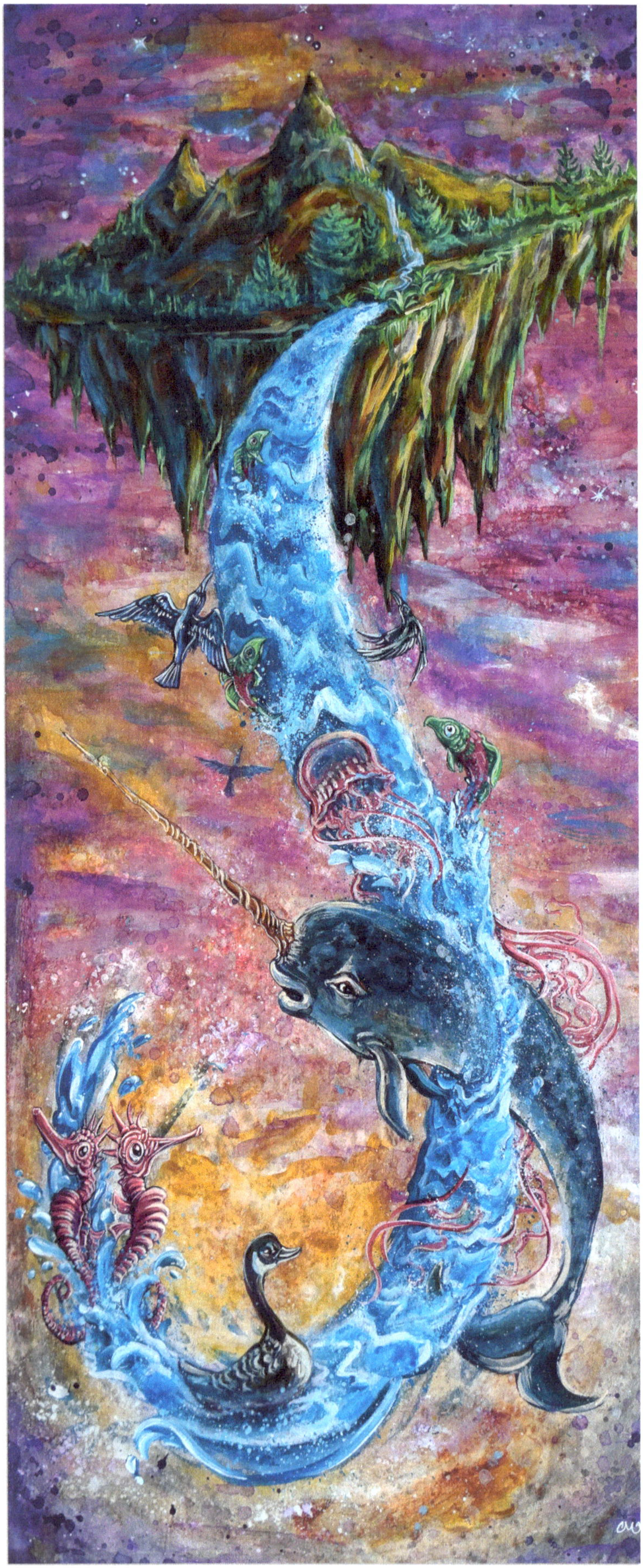

Persistence of Time

Life giving water.
Acrylic on wood 12"x24"

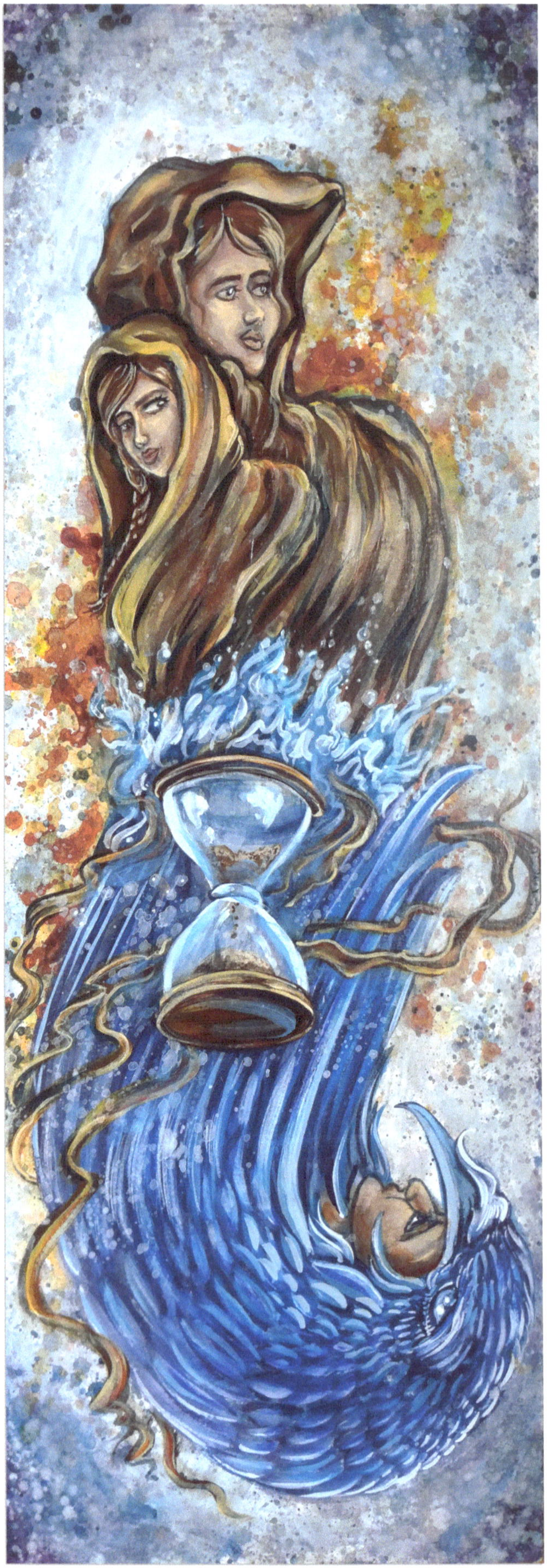

Time moves forward, the void grows closer,
it's nothing to fear.
Acrylic on wood 8"x24"

Mother Wolf

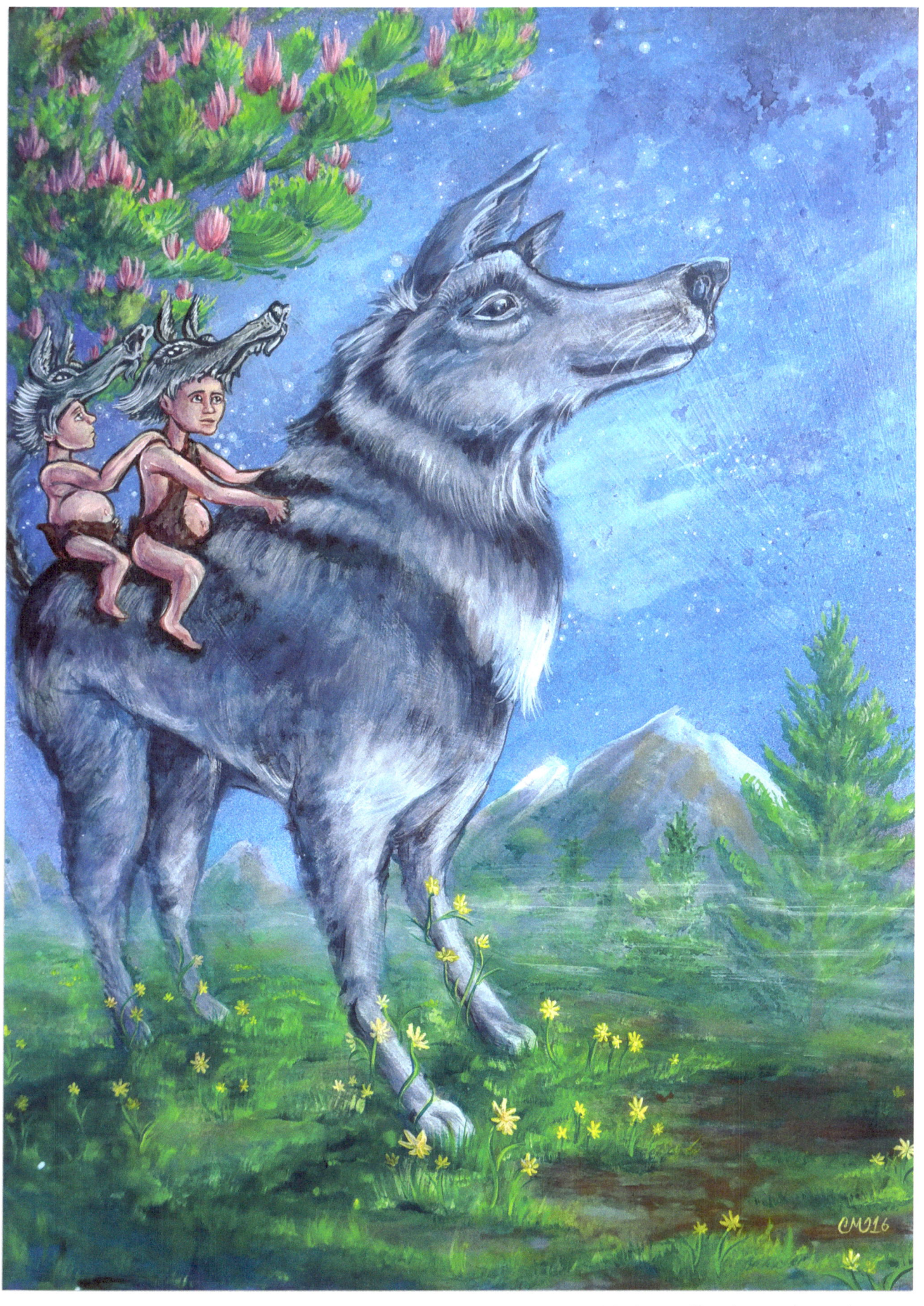

Mother wolf with Romulus and Remus.
Acrylic on wood 16"x20"

Exploring the Infinite Abyss of Introspection

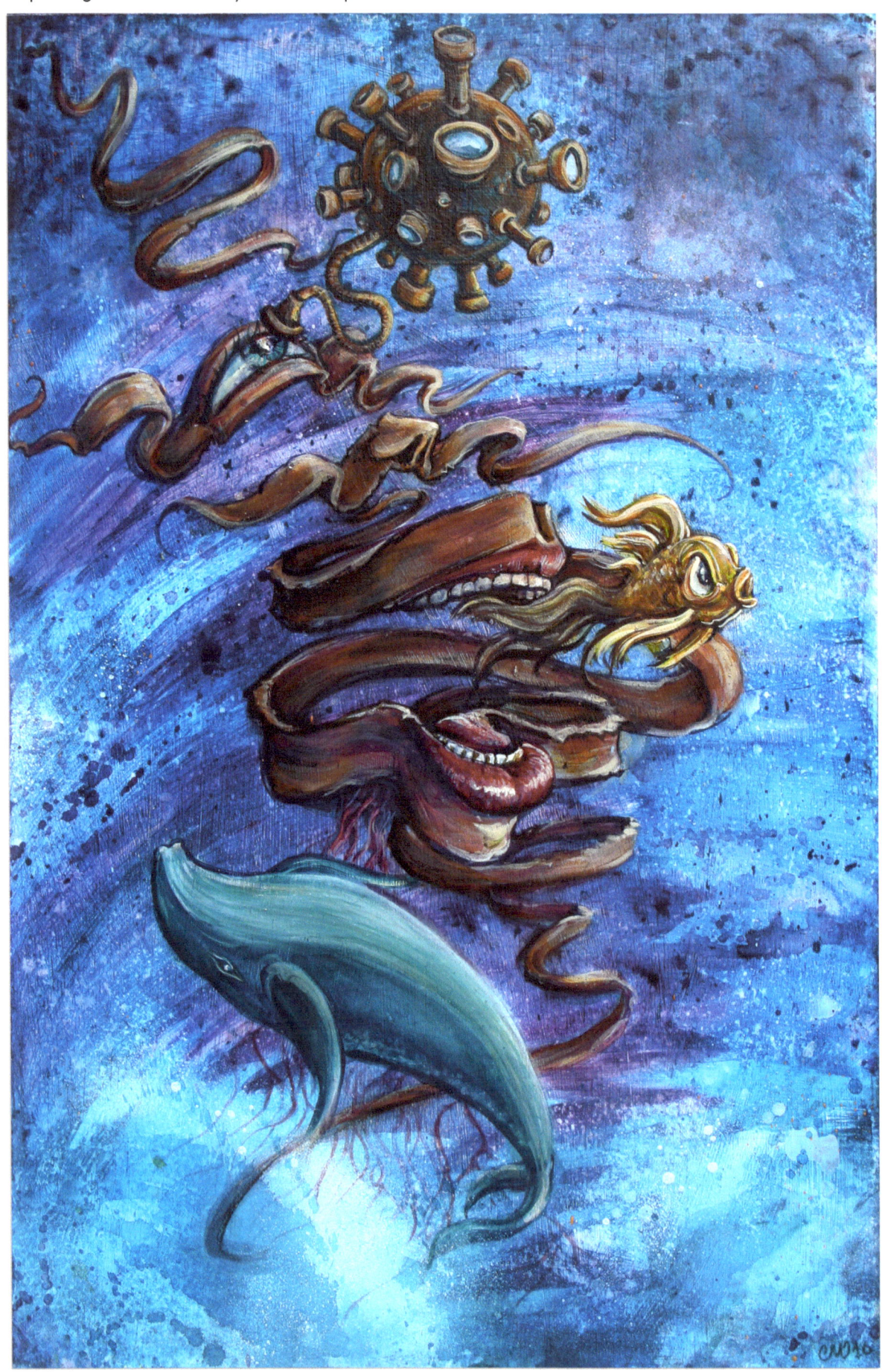

Introspection holds many perspectives, how deep do we go?
Acrylic on wood 16"x24"

Treasure Untold

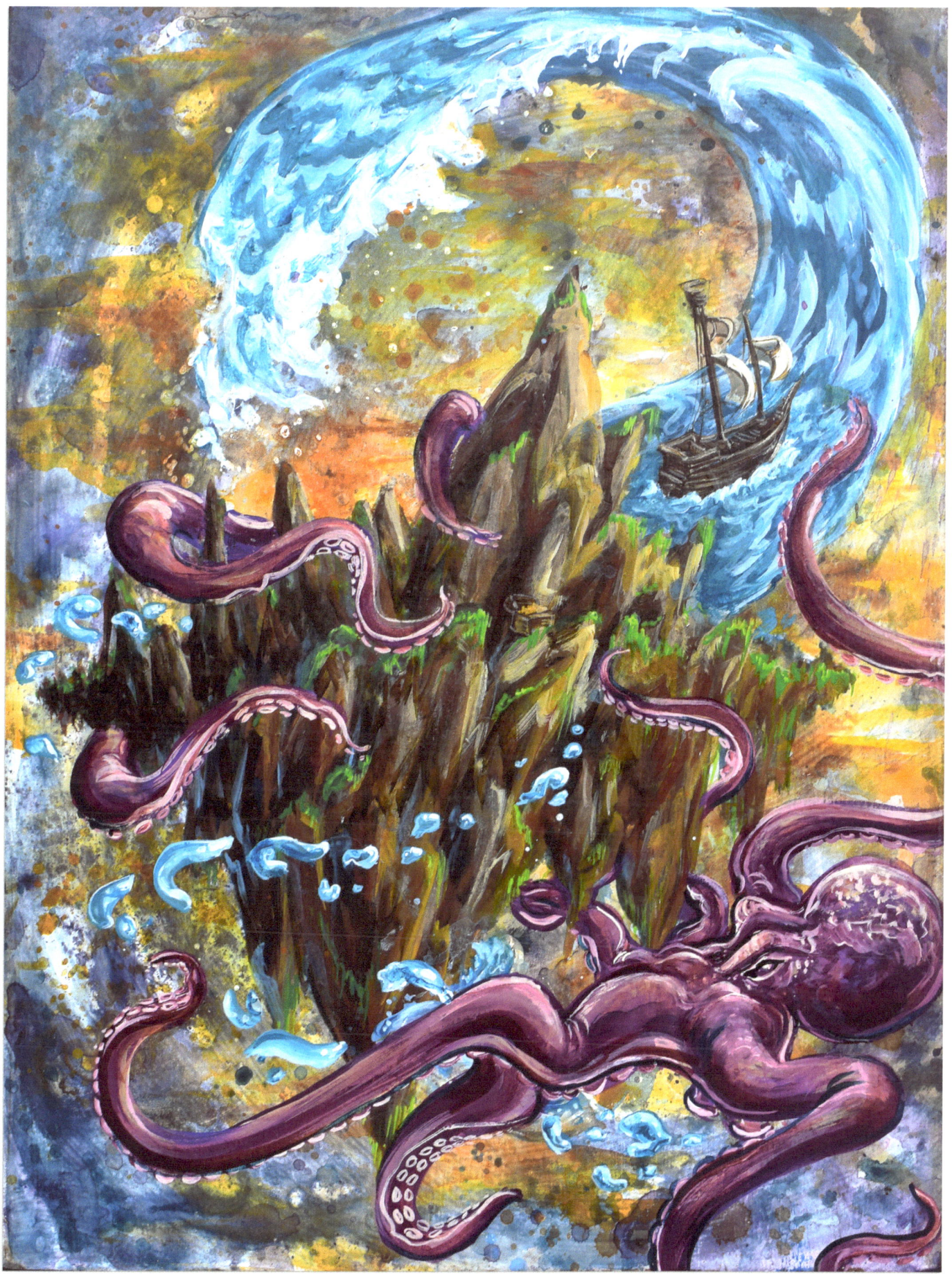

The biggest rewards often hold the most perilous journey. Often the voyage itself is a treasure.
Acrylic on wood 9"x12"

Blood Imbued with Rock and Wood

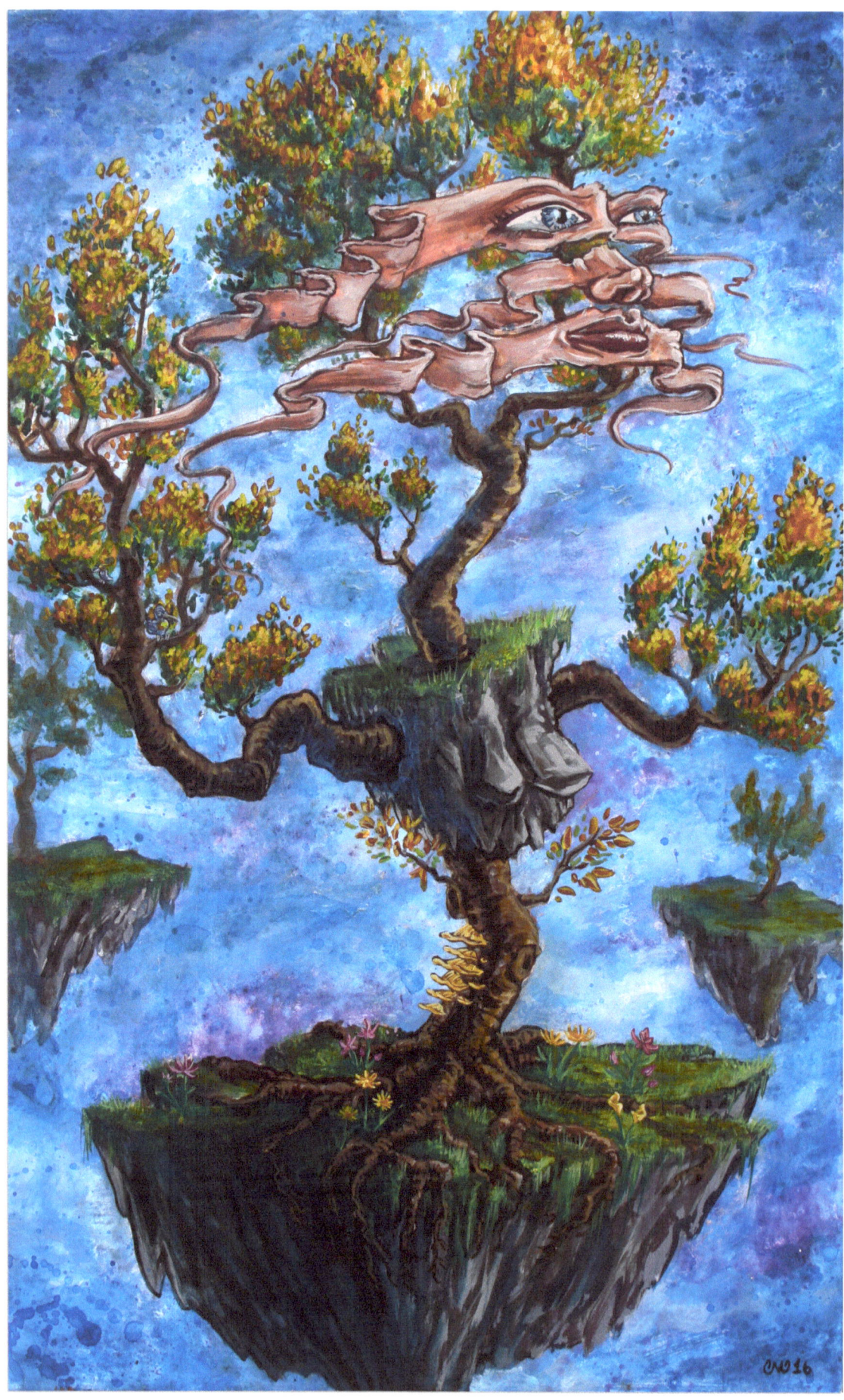

Feeling nature flow through our veins.
Acrylic on wood 16"x24"

Special Place

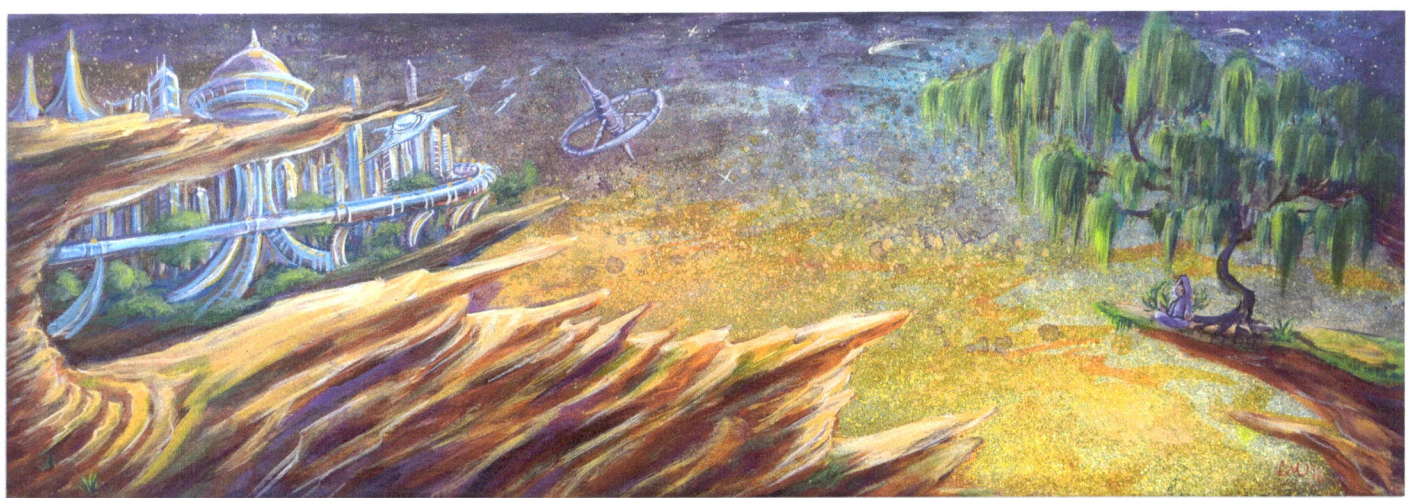

Finding a special place to meditate in a quickly evolving world.
Acrylic and spray paint on wood 6"x24"

Lifeblood

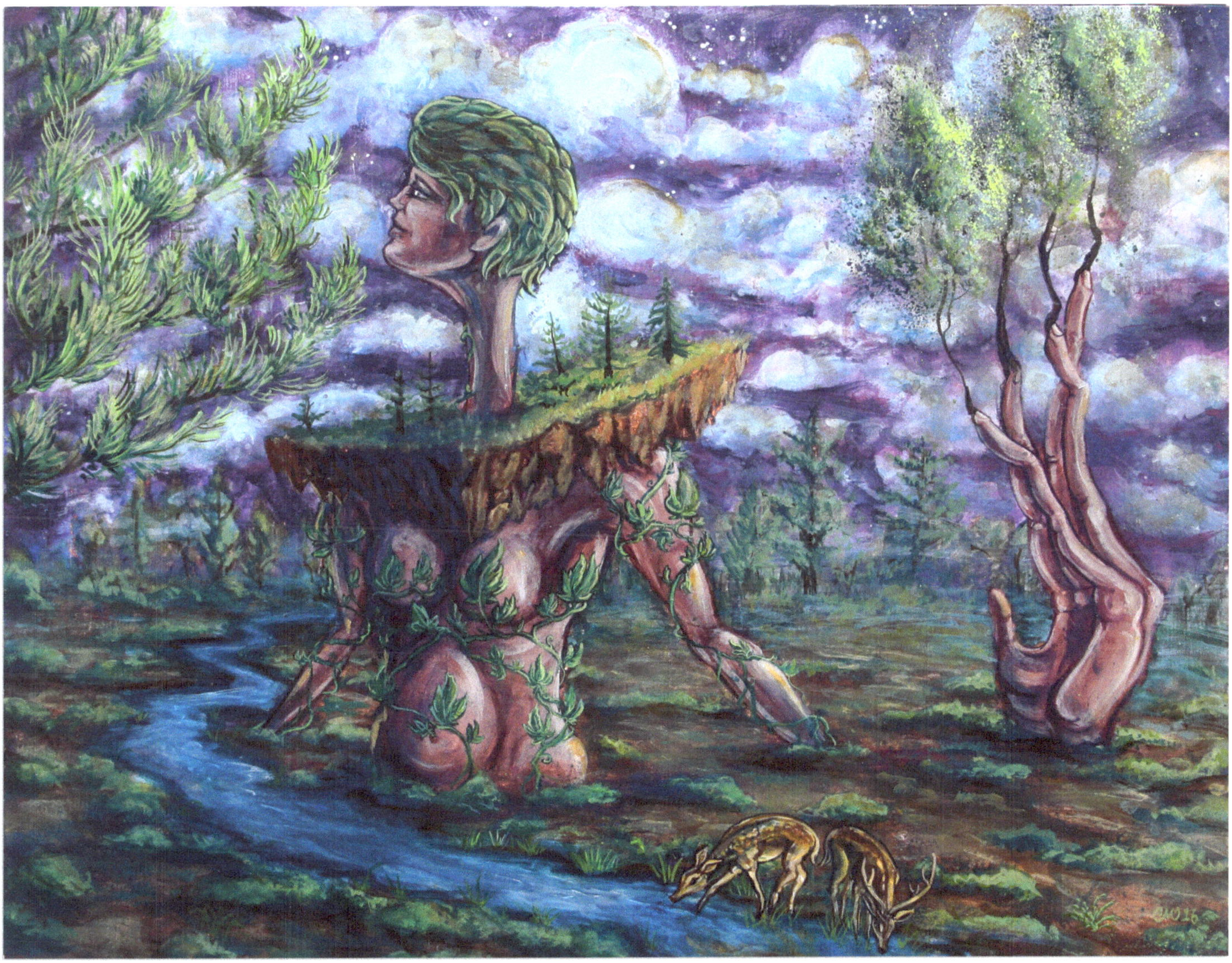

After making some work to fund raise for the Dakota pipeline protest, the importance of water became prominent in my work.
Acrylic on wood 16"x20"

Symbiotic

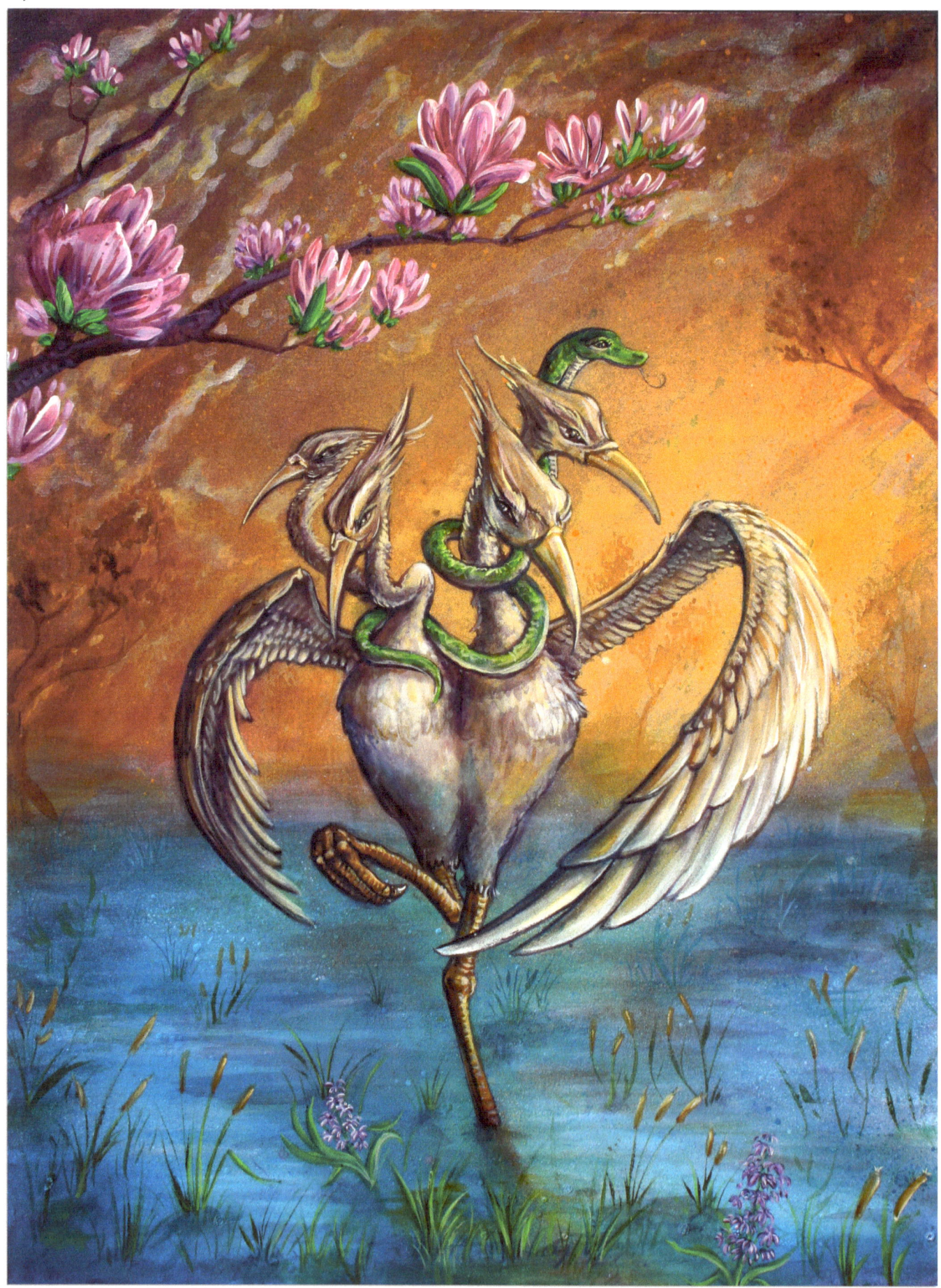

Predator prey relationships typically seen as being at odds, at times end up being symbiotic.
Acrylic on wood 18"x24"

Amethyst Falls

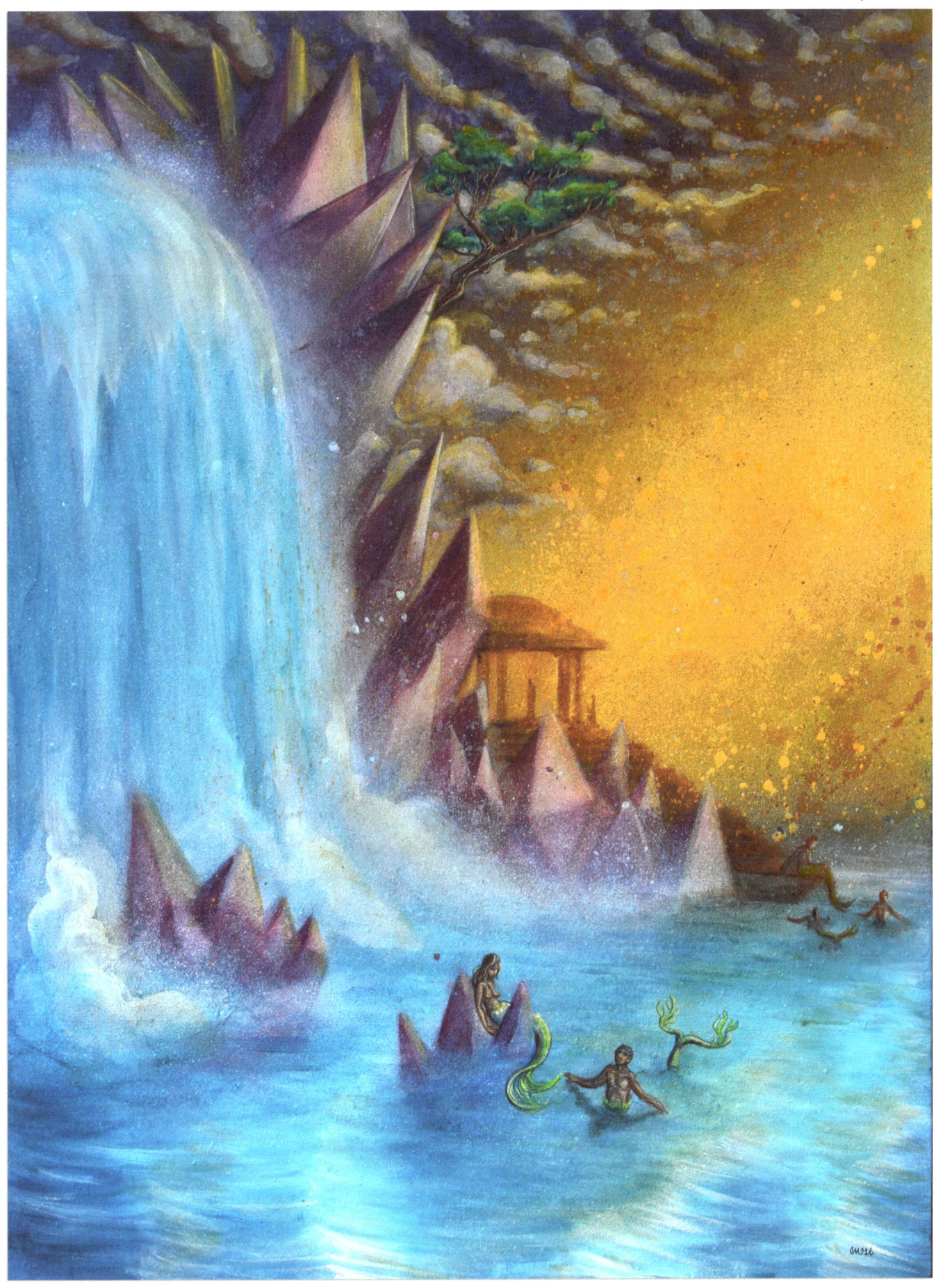

Sometimes I begin a background with the intention of it supporting a larger focal point or character, Sometimes the background wants to be the focal point. Amethyst Falls feels like an enchanted swimming hole.

Acrylic on wood 18"x24"

Mother Dearth

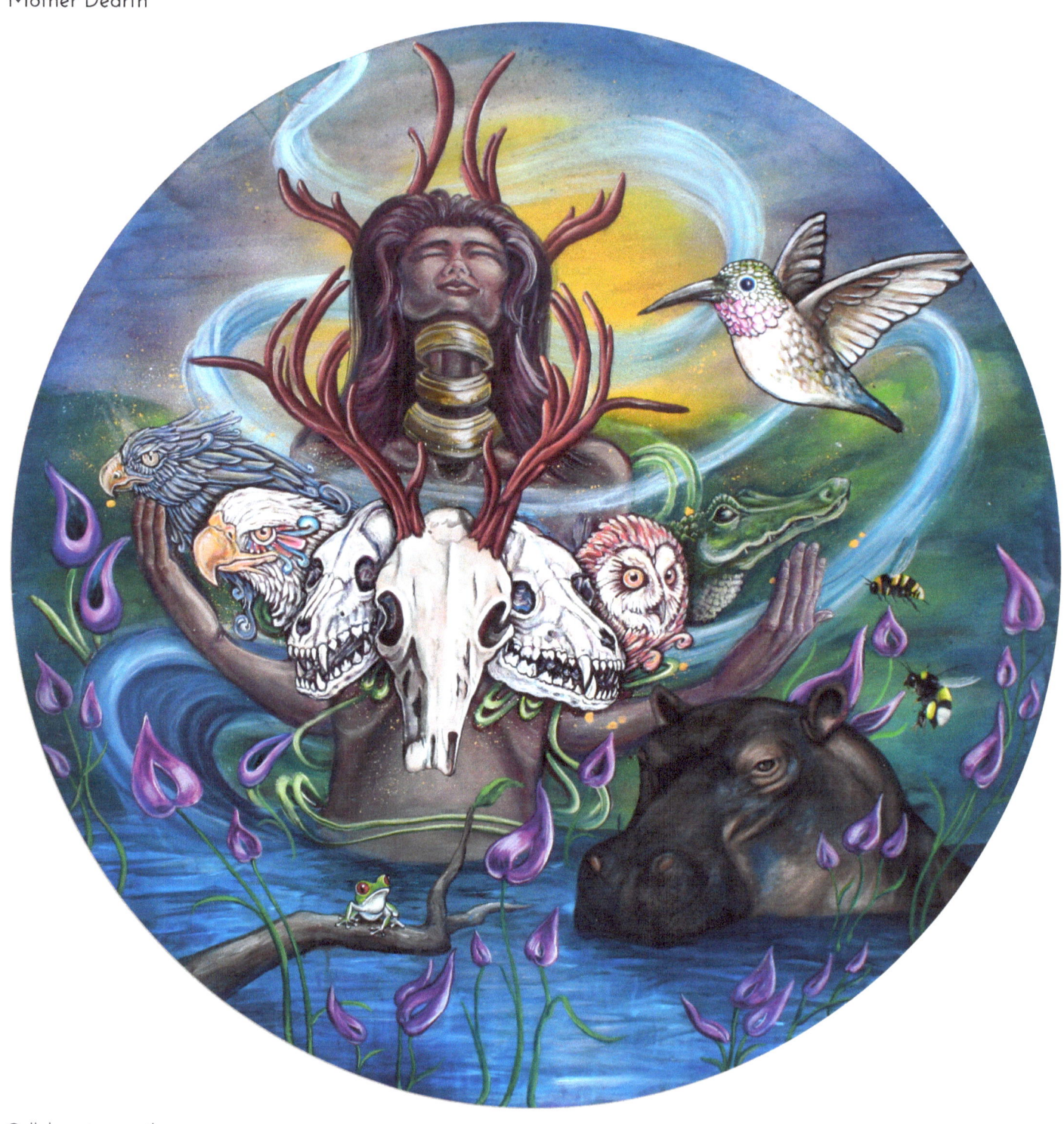

Collaboration with:
Emily Bates
Ali Schlicting
Jen Griffo
Matt Schlosky
Christopher Creath
Acrylic on 47" wood round

Re-Emergence

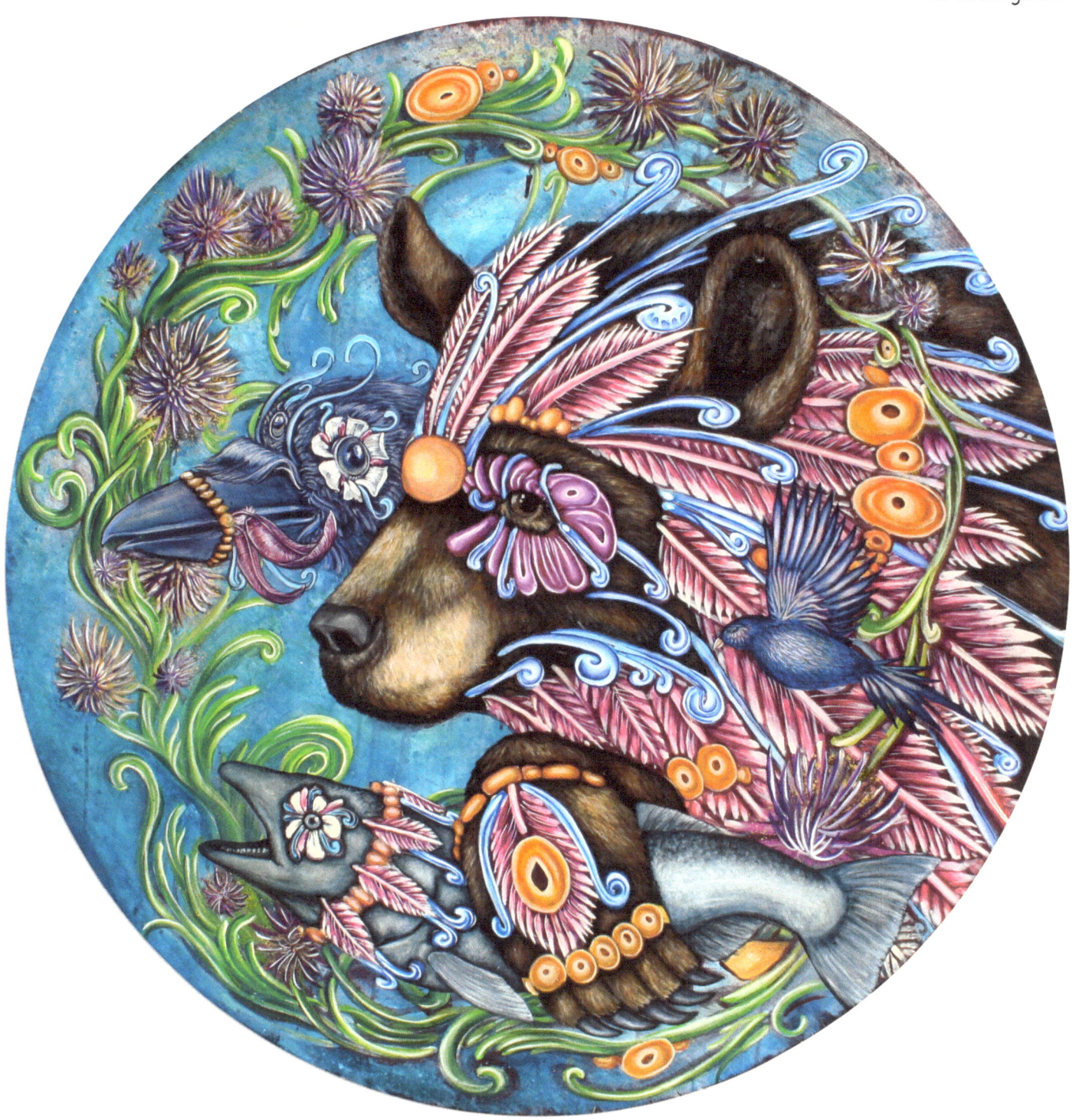

Collaboration with:
Emily Bates
Jen Griffo
Matt Schlosky
Christopher Creath
Acrylic on 47" wood round

Exploring Extremes and In-Betweens

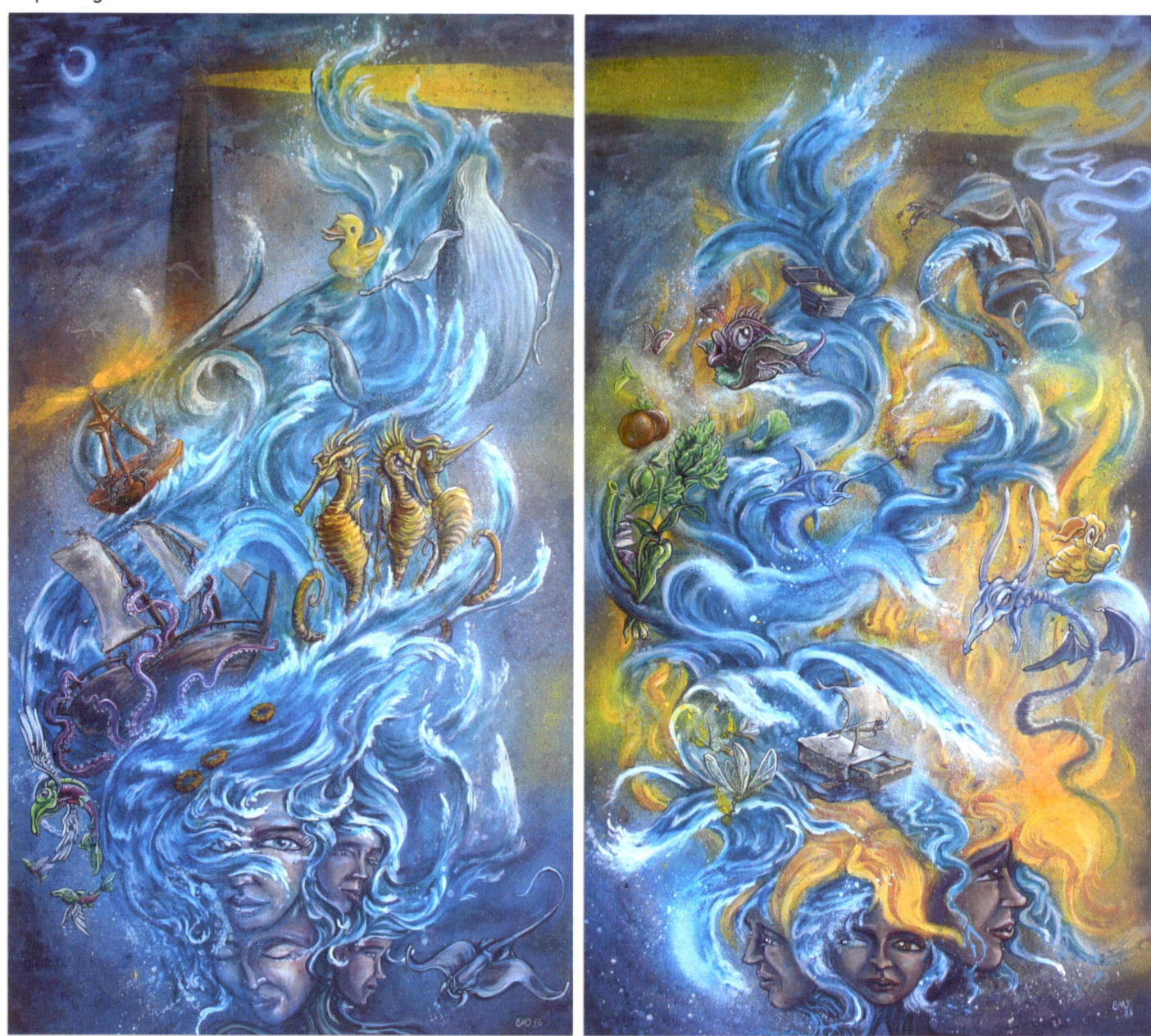

The pursuit of balance. This is a very personal piece for me, as it explores the concept of finding balance which has been a central part of my entire life, though not something I have always been able to achieve. On the left, the exploration of of the depths of introspection, and sometimes the feeling of despair, sadness, or loss. Also, the revelations, and motivation this can bring. In the middle is the attempts of finding balance, nurturing inspiration, healthy exploration. On the right, we have the fire, the drive, the mania. Creation and destruction. The Jack pines need fire to open their pine cones reproduce, and the Jack Pine Warbler need the young jack pines for their nest. Finding balance can sometimes be a tumultuous thing, but knowing that the light and dark, highs and lows are part of the path, helps me to recognize the need to not stay on one side too long.
Acrylic on wood (3) 36"x48"

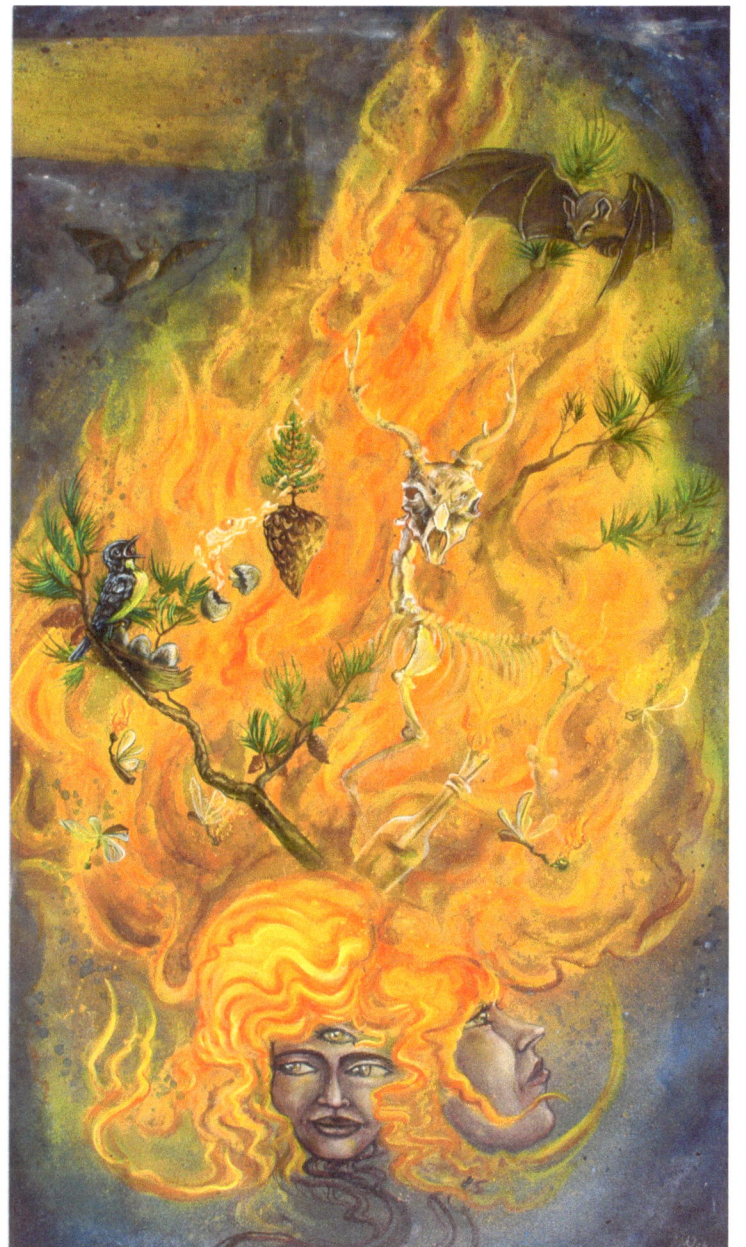

Hearts-a-Flood Mind-a-Flutter

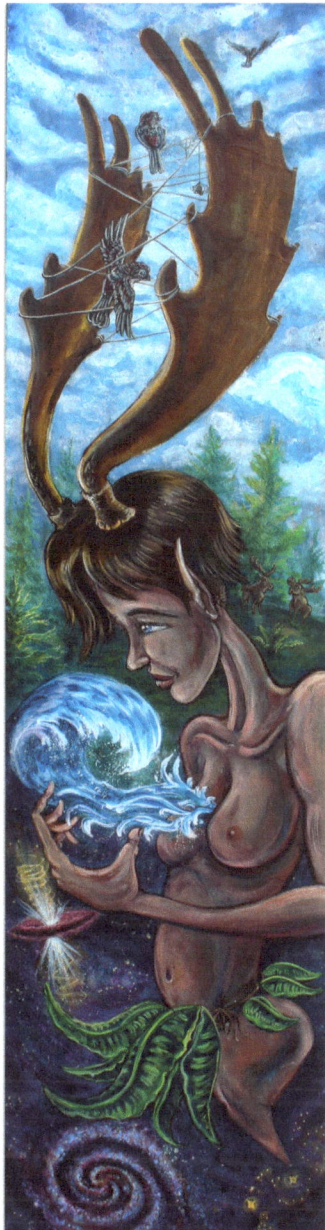

The moments with a full heart
and mind a flutter with ideas.
Acrylic on wood 12"x48"

Impulse to Action

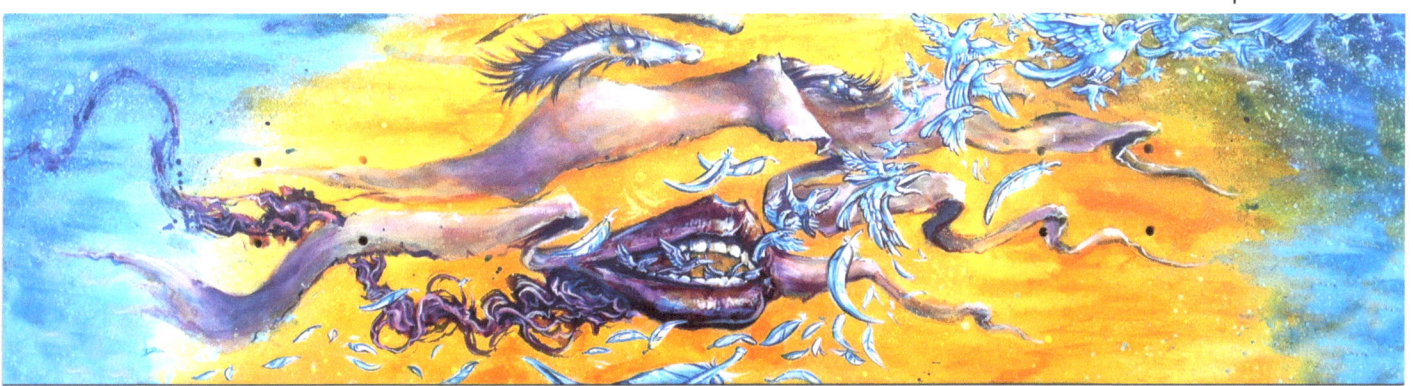

Electric signals through our nerves creating actions. Making sure the words se are well consdiered help shape a more positive reality.
Acrylic and spray paint on wood skate board 8"x32"

Arrow

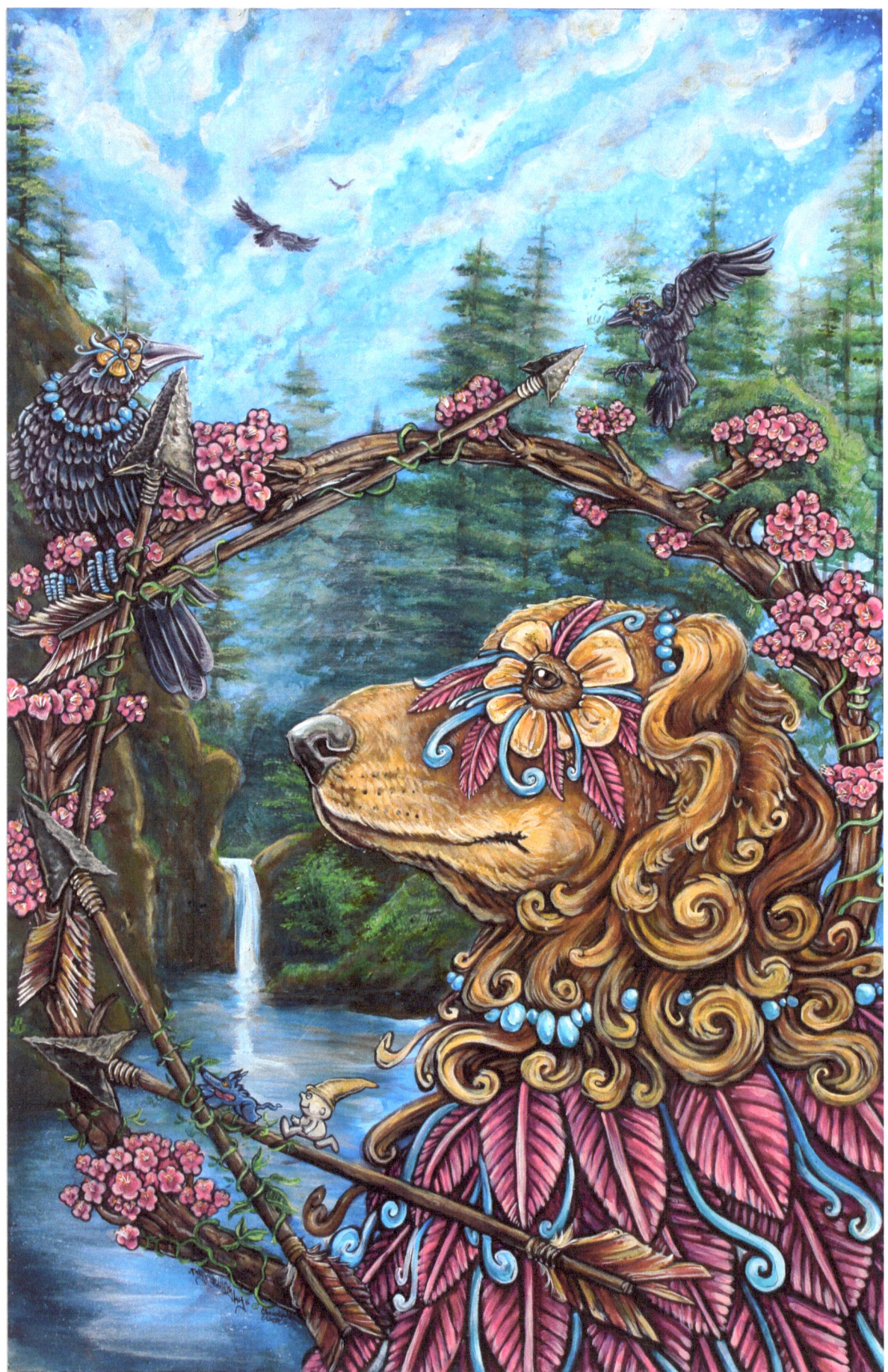

A collaboration with Matt Schlosky and Christopher Creath to pay pay tribute to a special golden retriever named after "Arrow" from the film "The Point" who really enjoyed hikes to Punch Bowl Falls in Oregon.
Acrylic on wood 24"x36"

Divergent Interpretations of a Singular Intention

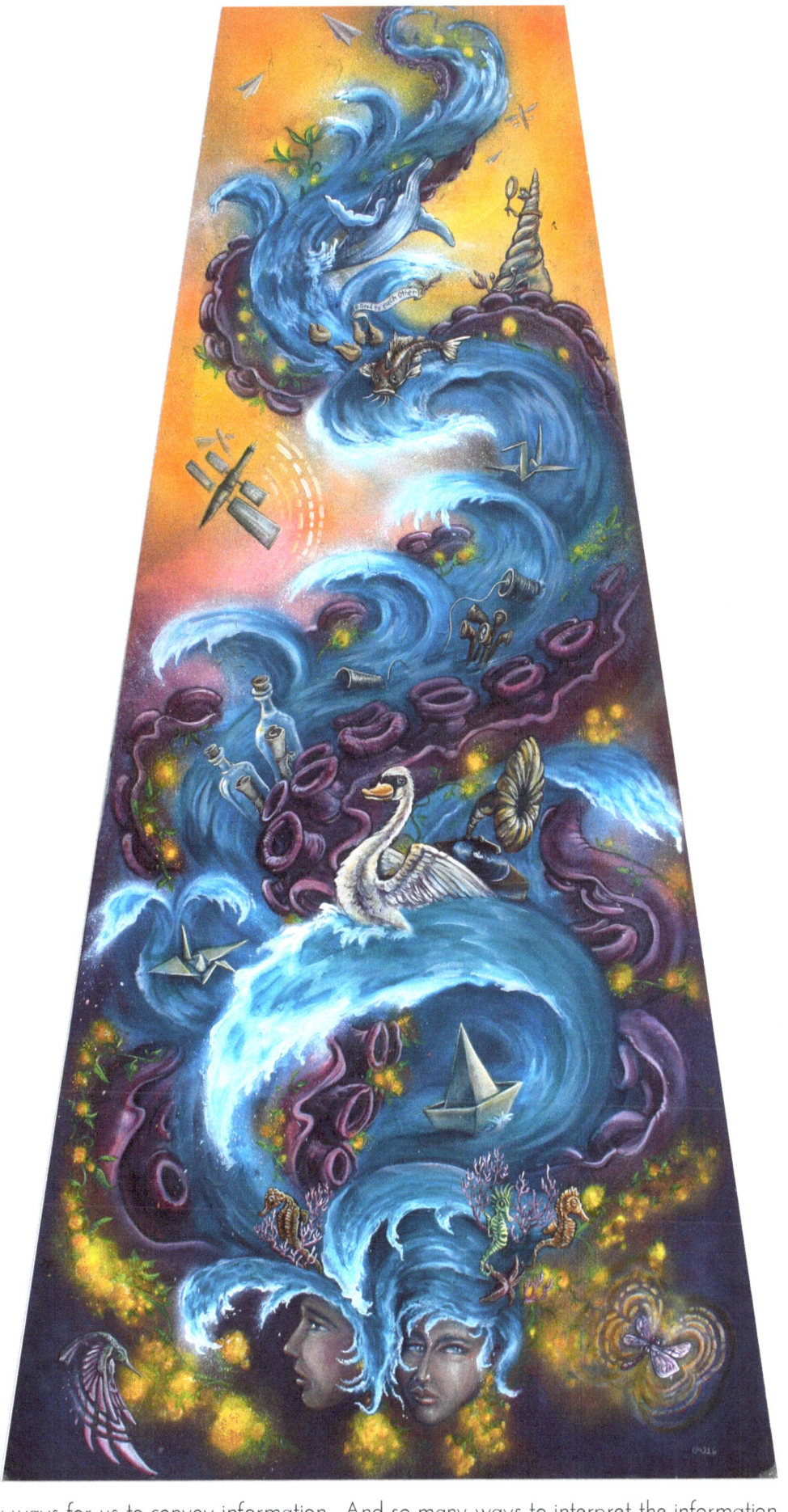

So many ways for us to convey information... And so many ways to interpret the information.

Acrylic on wood 48"x84"

Indigenous

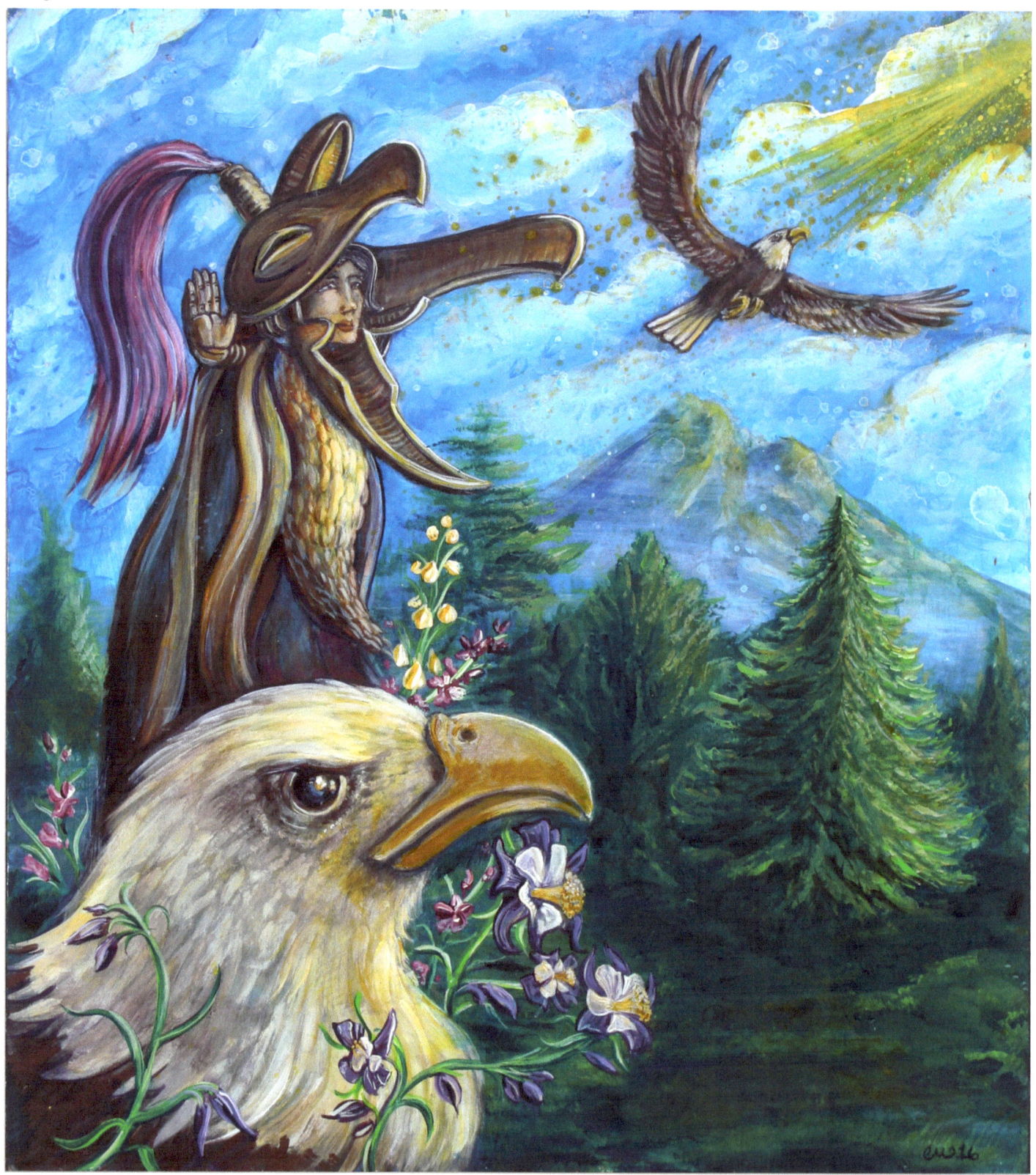

Inspired by the exhibition at the Portland Art Museum displaying the indigenous art of the Pacific Northwest.
Acrylic on wood 14"x16"

Valhalla Dreamin'

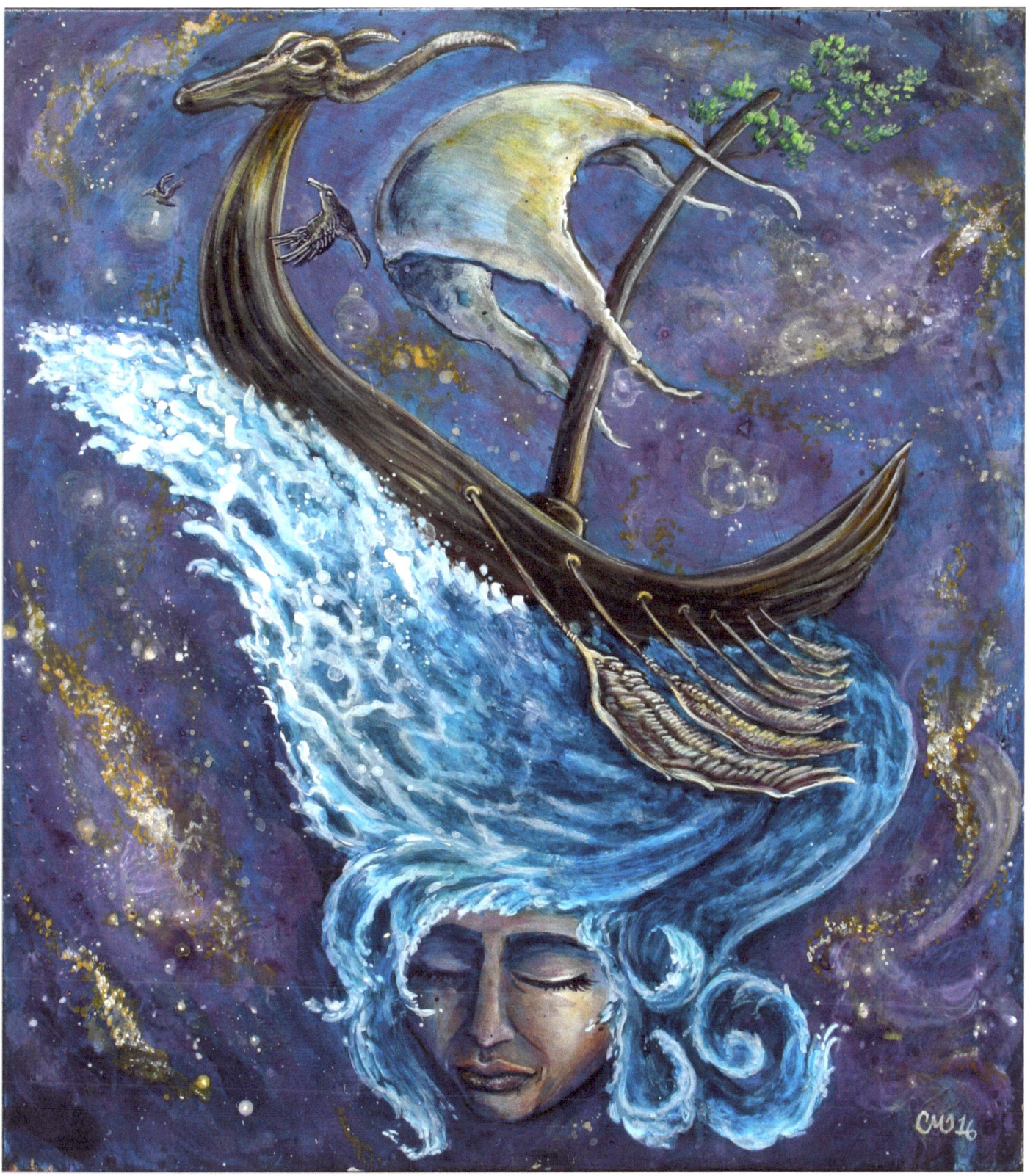

Setting sail on a cerebral sea, imagining the afterlife.
Acrylic on wood 16"x20"

Standing Bear

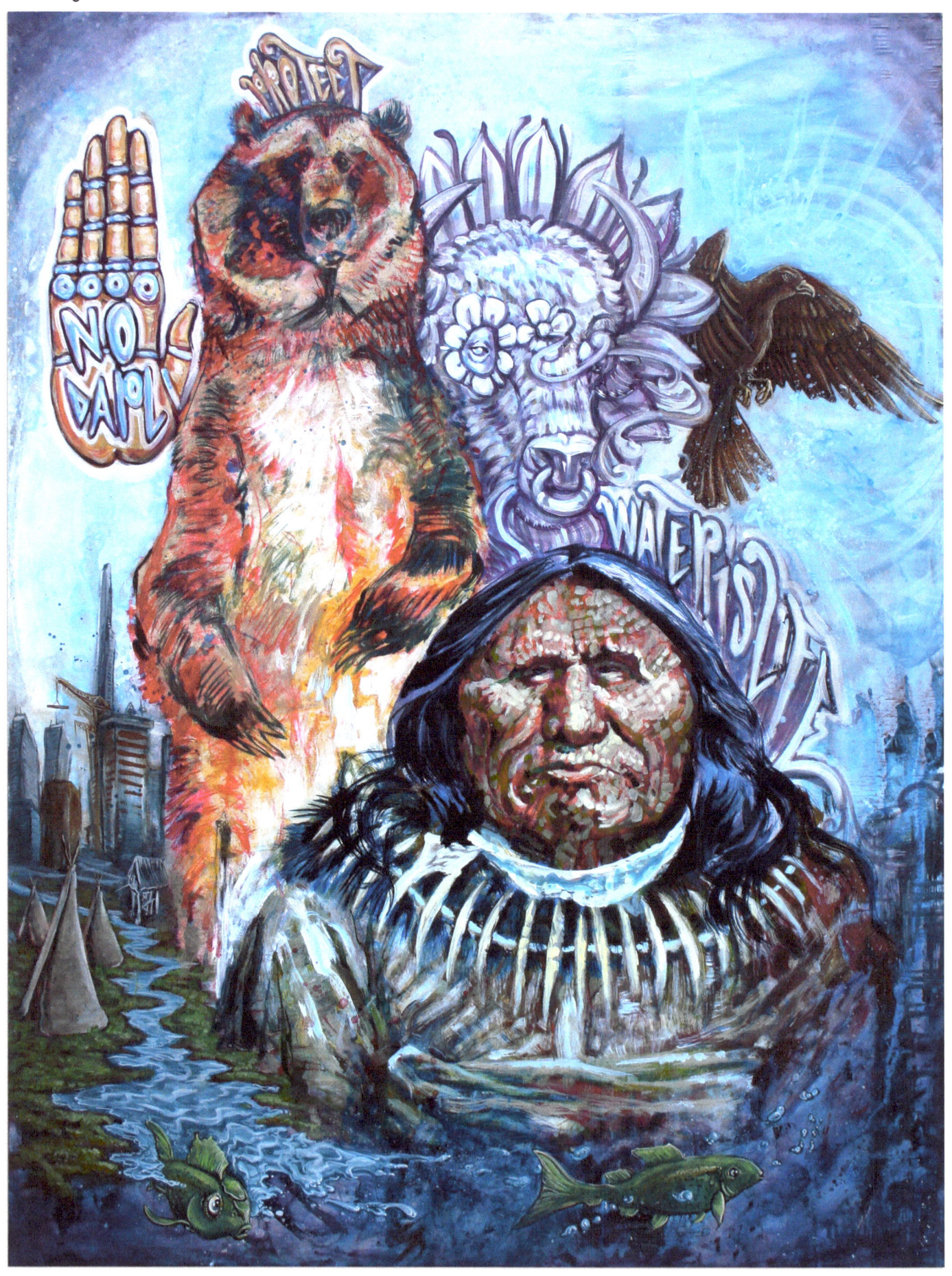

Collaboration with Sam Arneson and Matt Schlosky and Christopher Creath created to rasie awareness and funds for the No DAPL legal fund.
Acrylic on wood 36"x48"

Water is Life

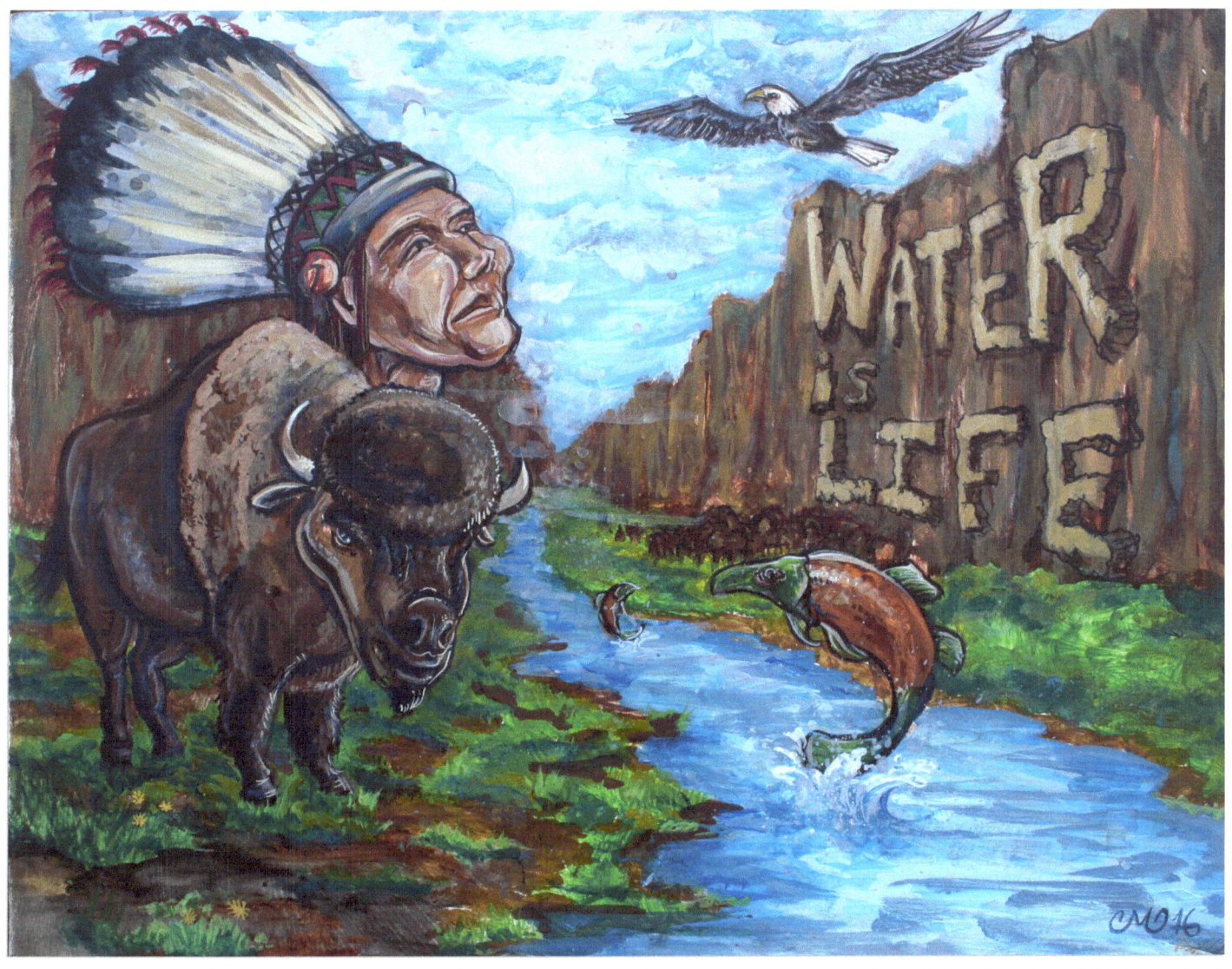

Created to pay homage to the life giving water and to raise awareness and funds for the No DAPL legal fund.
Acrylic on wood 9"x12"

The Ubiquitous Experience Album Cover

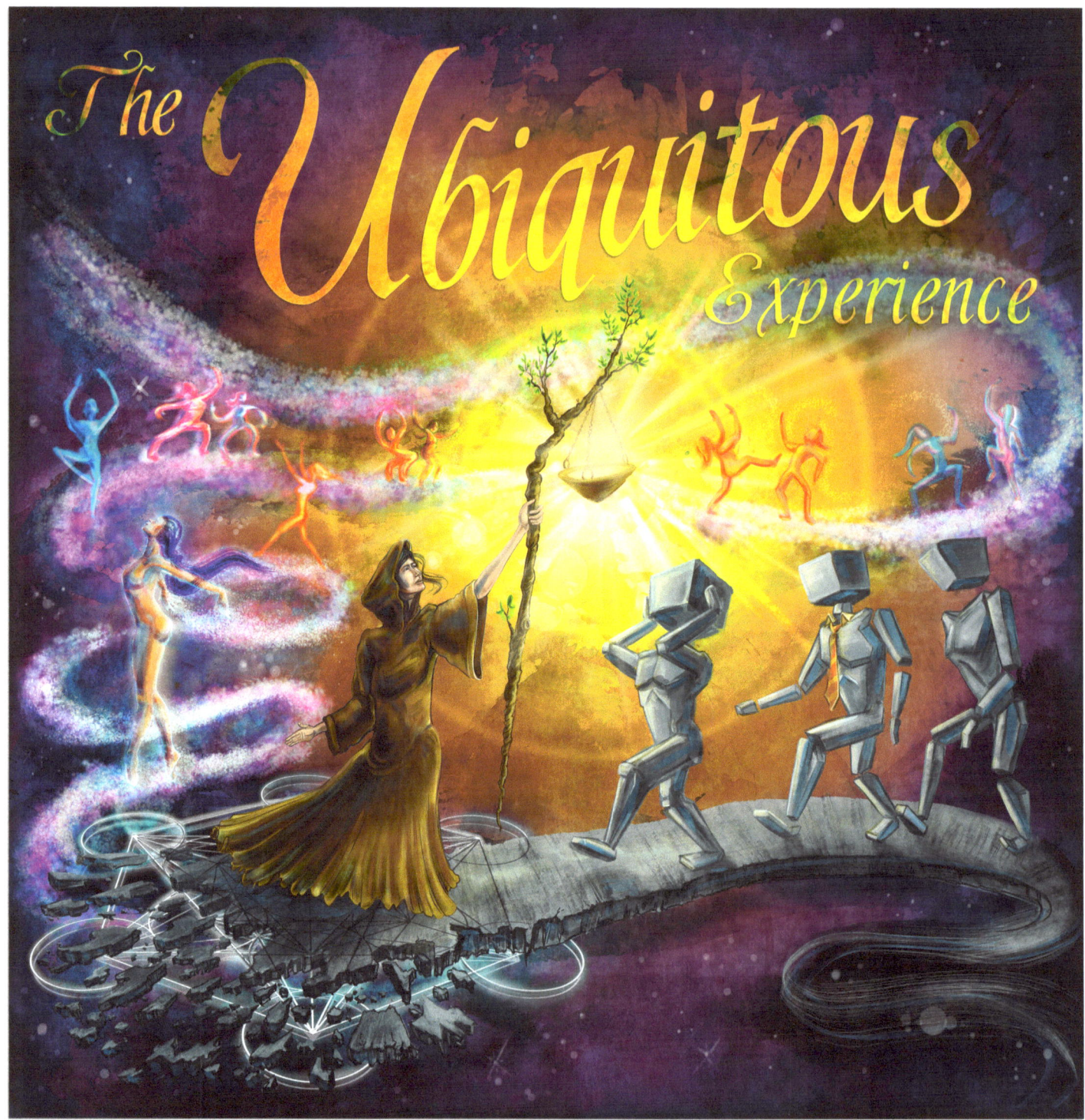

The gatekeeper shattering antiquated paradigms allowing the block people to live free.
Created with Painter and Photoshop

Creating our Creation Tales

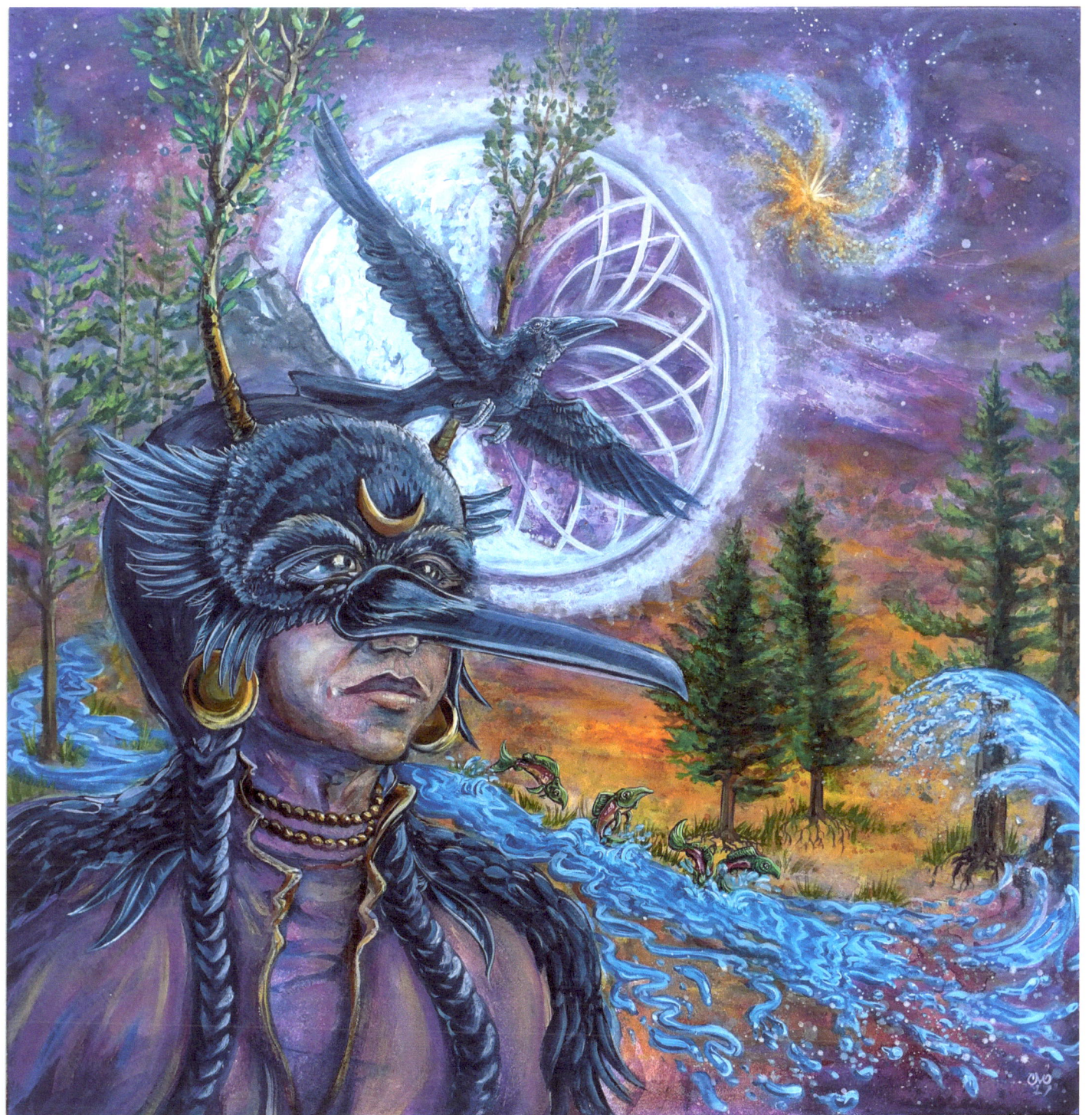

What would your creation tale sound like?

Icy

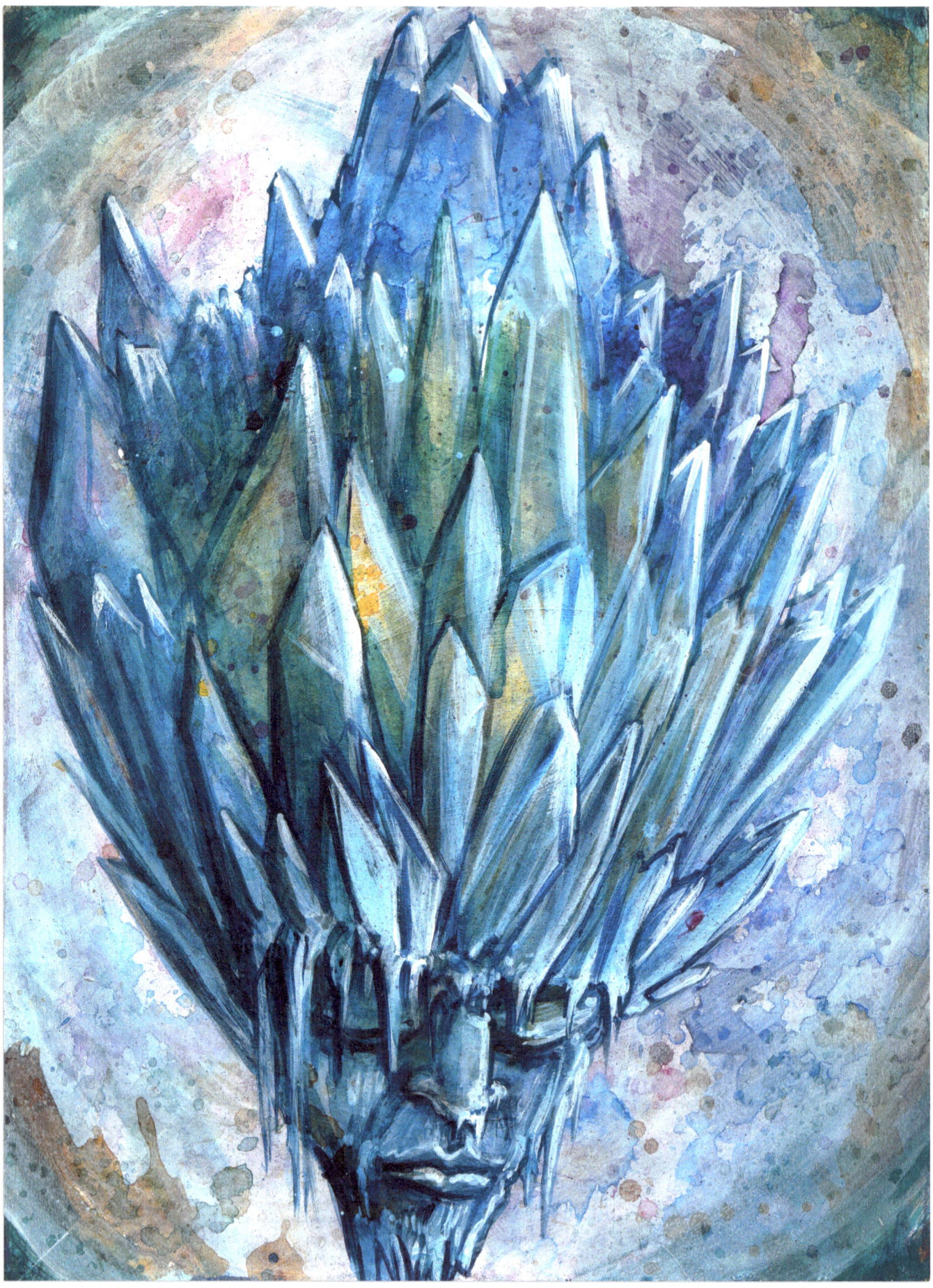

The winter was frosty this year.
Acrylic on wood 9"x12"

Eternal Optimist

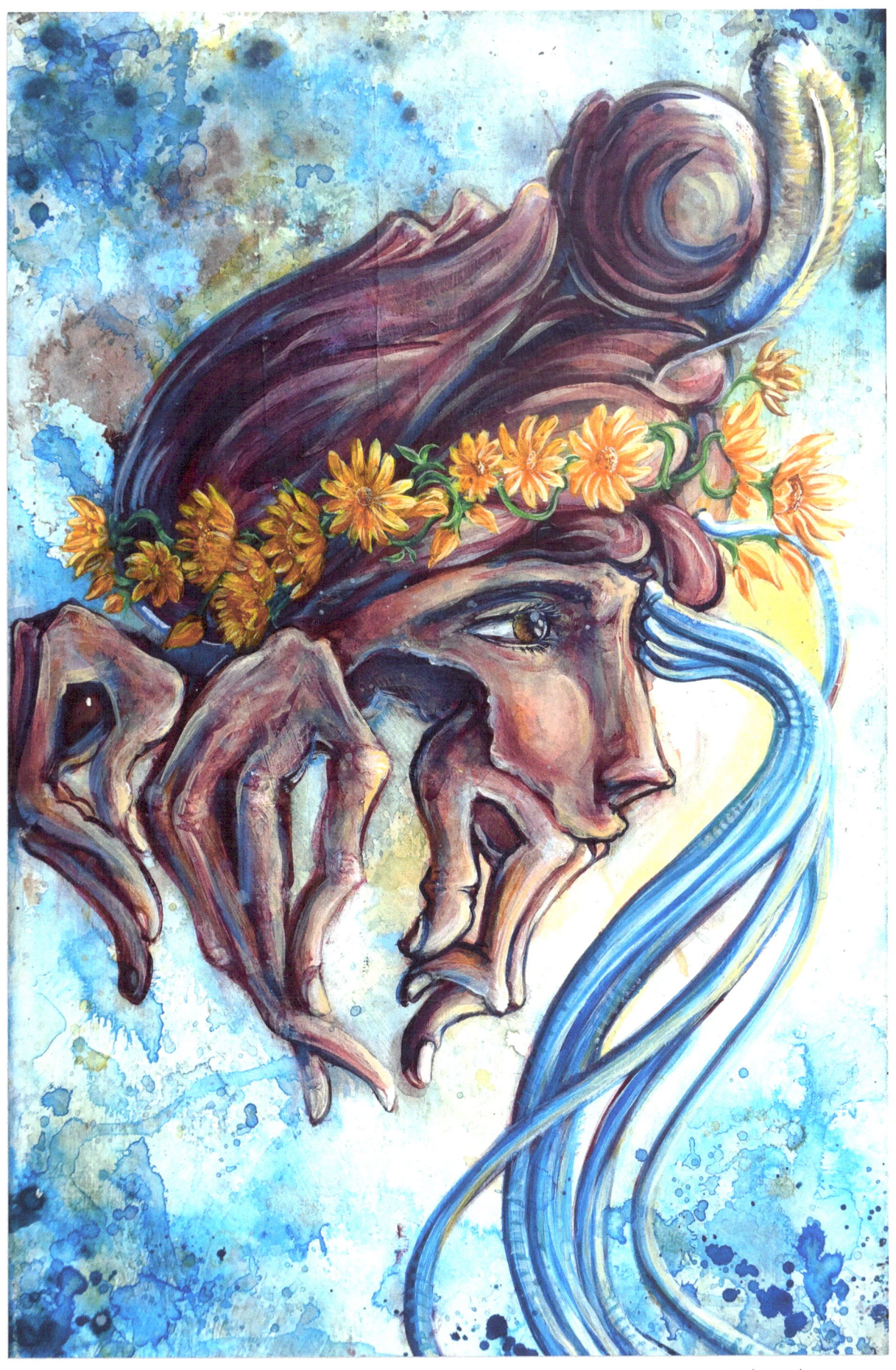

Hardwired optimism.
Acrylic on wood 12"x16"

The Ubiquitous Experience Cover

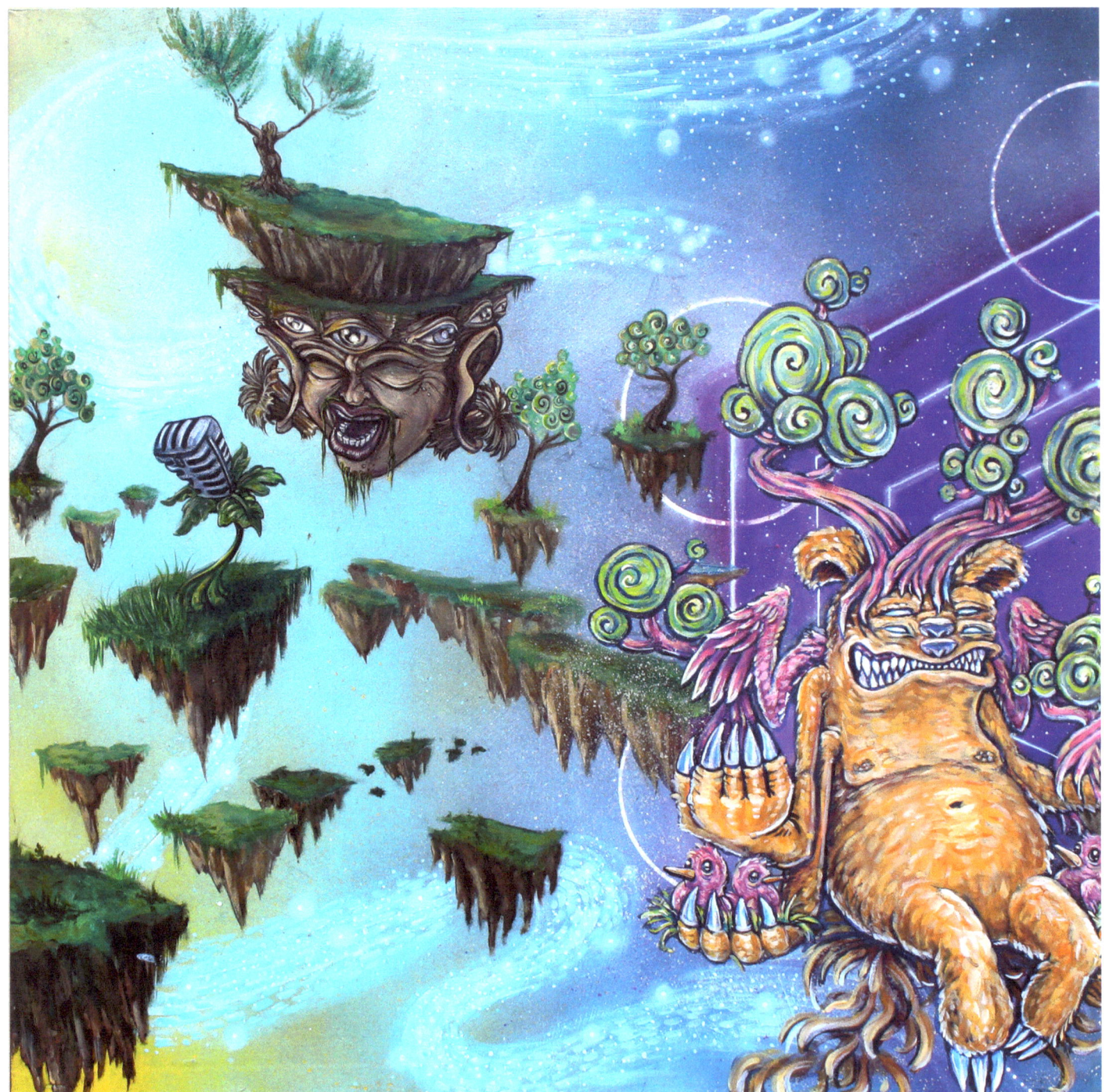

Collaboration with Nathan Turner, Matt Schlosky, and Christopher Creath. Created for the band "The Ubiquitous Experience"
Acrylic and spray paint on wood (2) 24"x24"

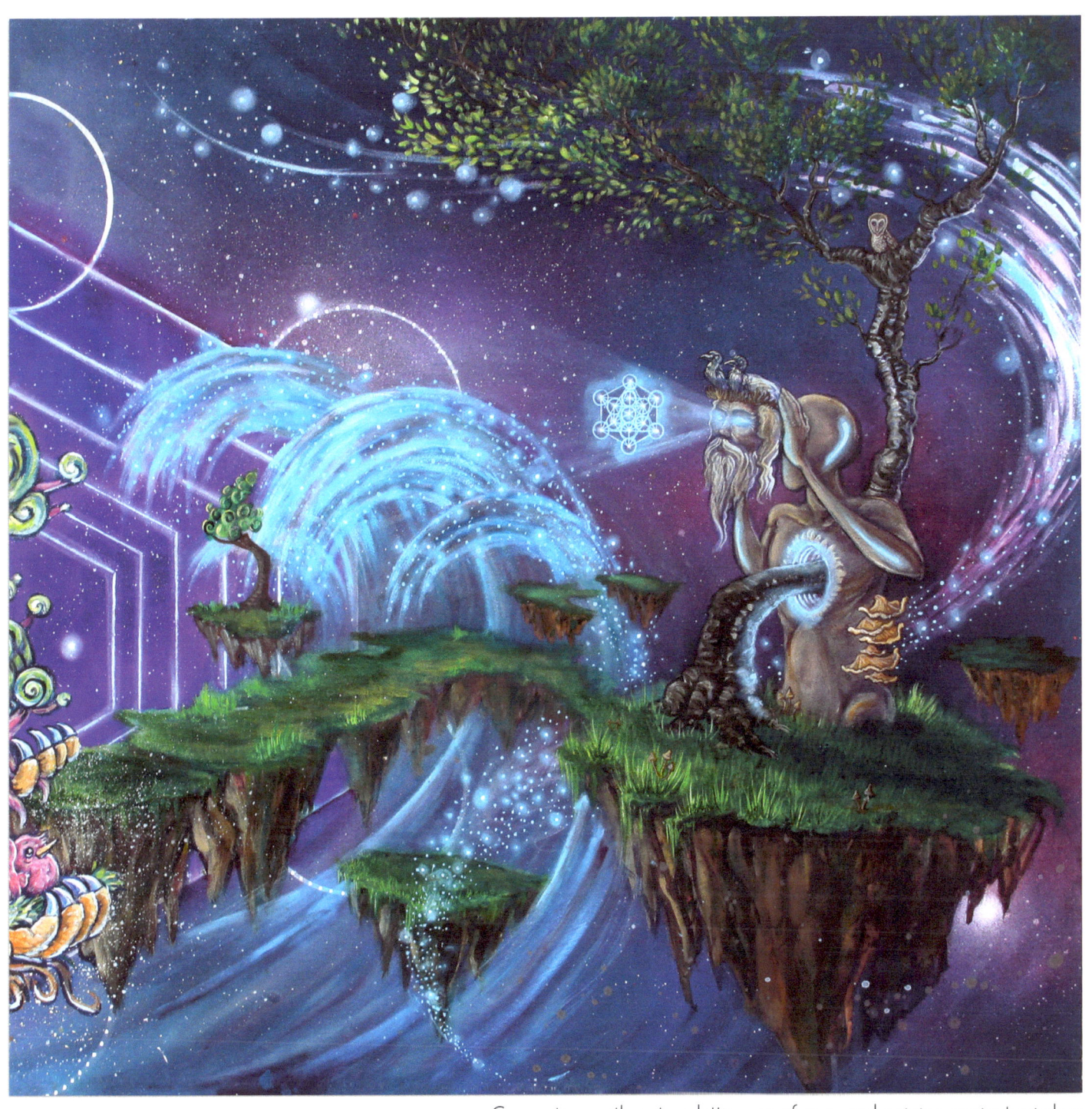

Connecting with nature letting go of ego, and gaining ancient wisdom.

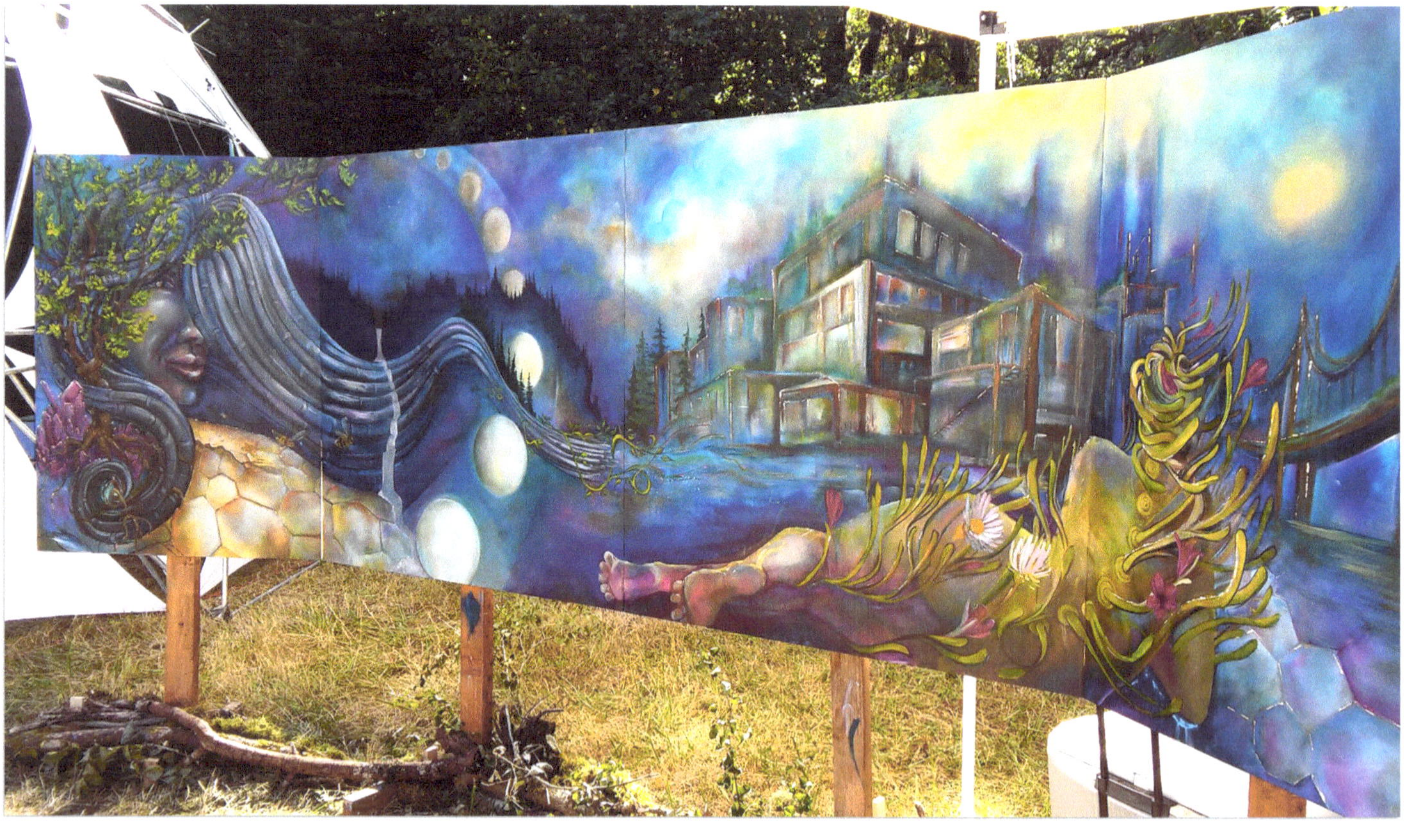

Reciprocation

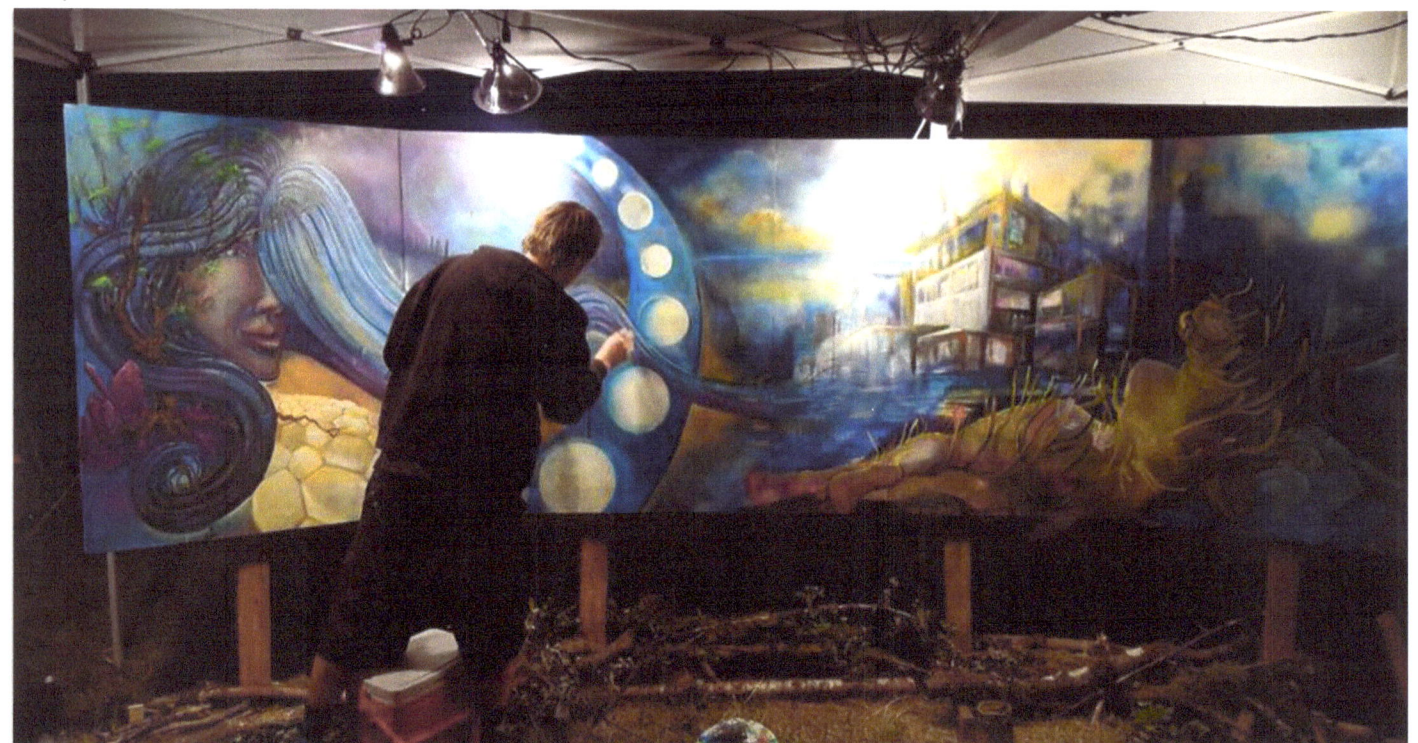

Collaborative live painting at "Human Nature" 2015 with Kaitlyn Mckenzie Nelson, Michelle Purvis, Kirsten Muir, and Christopher Creath Curated by Bea Ogden of Cloud Break Portland Oregon
Acrylic and spraypaint on wood 156"x48

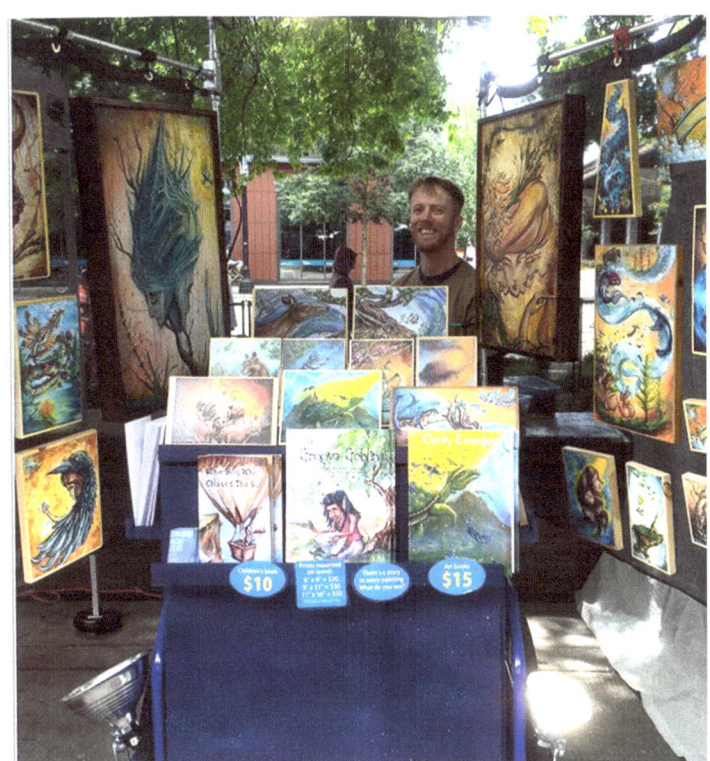 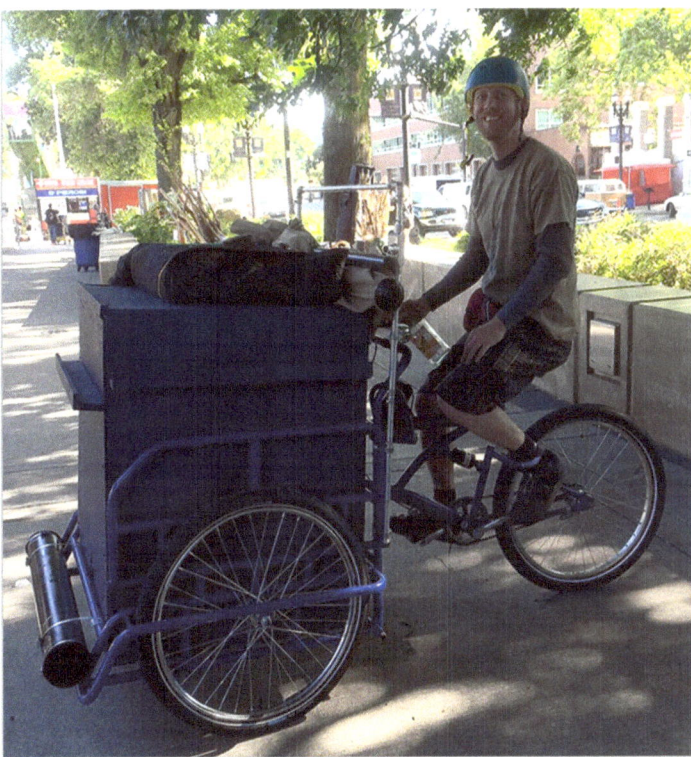

Mobile Art vending setup at the Portland Saturday Market

Over the past few years I have had the pleasure of taking my art directly to my audience through art fairs and making Portland Saturday market my homebase. This group of paintings is the majority of the work made in 2016-2017, and is the third installment of art books I have created. The other two books "Incoherent Insight" 2013, and "Clarity Emerging" 2016 are collections of work that emerged from a need to deal with some inner turmoil. Although challenges are ever present, I believe my ability to stay relatively centered, in stormy seas has allowed me to create a body of work that can be less influenced by turbulence, and more open to divine inspiration. Not having a set process to follow, I tend to try and keep it experimental and spontaneous, in order to remain open to the delicate whisper of the muses. A good portion of the work has aspirations of connecting with nature, as this is where I find the inspiration strongest. I am very grateful for my supportive audience, thank you! I hope you enjoyed the book.

More of my work can be found at www.ChristopherCreath.com

www.ingramcontent.com/pod-product-compliance
Lightning Source LLC
Chambersburg PA
CBHW040452220526
45473CB00004B/1610